Cambridge Lower Secondary
English
WORKBOOK 7

Graham Elsdon with Esther Menon

CAMBRIDGE
UNIVERSITY PRESS

Shaftesbury Road, Cambridge CB2 8EA, United Kingdom

One Liberty Plaza, 20th Floor, New York, NY 10006, USA

477 Williamstown Road, Port Melbourne, VIC 3207, Australia

314–321, 3rd Floor, Plot 3, Splendor Forum, Jasola District Centre, New Delhi – 110025, India

103 Penang Road, #05-06/07, Visioncrest Commercial, Singapore 238467

Cambridge University Press is part of the University of Cambridge.

It furthers the University's mission by disseminating knowledge in the pursuit of education, learning and research at the highest international levels of excellence.

www.cambridge.org
Information on this title: www.cambridge.org/9781108746625

© Cambridge University Press & Assessment 2021

This publication is in copyright. Subject to statutory exception and to the provisions of relevant collective licensing agreements, no reproduction of any part may take place without the written permission of Cambridge University Press.

First published 2012
Second edition 2021

20 19 18 17 16 15 14 13 12 11 10 9 8 7 6

Printed in Malaysia by Vivar Printing

A catalogue record for this publication is available from the British Library

ISBN 978-1-108-74662-5 Paperback with Digital Access (1 Year)

Cambridge University Press has no responsibility for the persistence or accuracy of URLs for external or third-party internet websites referred to in this publication, and does not guarantee that any content on such websites is, or will remain, accurate or appropriate. Information regarding prices, travel timetables, and other factual information given in this work is correct at the time of first printing but Cambridge University Press does not guarantee the accuracy of such information thereafter.

....

NOTICE TO TEACHERS IN THE UK
It is illegal to reproduce any part of this work in material form (including photocopying and electronic storage) except under the following circumstances:
(i)   where you are abiding by a licence granted to your school or institution by the Copyright Licensing Agency;
(ii) where no such licence exists, or where you wish to exceed the terms of a licence, and you have gained the written permission of Cambridge University Press;
(iii) where you are allowed to reproduce without permission under the provisions of Chapter 3 of the Copyright, Designs and Patents Act 1988, which covers, for example, the reproduction of short passages within certain types of educational anthology and reproduction for the purposes of setting examination questions.

Third-party websites, publications and resources referred to in this publication have not been endorsed by Cambridge Assessment International Education.

Contents

1	Adventure	5
2	'Hey, You Down There'	19
3	Film and fame	31
4	Small but perfect	47
5	Unusual education	61
6	Life stories	74
7	'The Travel Agency'	90
8	In the city	104
9	Dangers of the sea	118

How to use this book

This workbook provides questions for you to practise what you have learnt in the Learner's Book. There is a unit to match each unit in your Learner's Book. Each session is divided into three parts:

Focus: these questions help you to master the basics

Focus

1   Here are three paragraphs from a short story about a sailor. In the right-hand column, note down what information is kept from the reader in each paragraph. The first one has been done for you.

Paragraph content	What information the reader doesn't know
1 A sailor receives a letter telling him to arrive at the harbour to get on his boat the following morning with a packed suitcase.	Who the sailor is; why he has been sent the letter; who has sent it.
2 The sailor meets a friend that evening. They talk about a dangerous sea captain they both know. The friend knows a secret about the sea captain.	
3 The next morning, the sea captain is waiting on the ship in the harbour. He has an angry look on his face. The sailor hasn't arrived.	

Practice: these questions help you to become more confident in using what you have learnt

Practice

2   Look at these headlines. Which of the techniques listed in Activity 1 are used here? Write the technique next to the headline. You may be able to see more than one technique in a headline.

a   NOT AT ALL FARE! ....

b   A shoal lot of fun... ....

c   Weird and wonderful Whales! ....

d   THE END OF THE MALE RACE AS WE KNOW IT? ....

Challenge: these questions will make you think hard

Challenge

3   In your notebook, write two paragraphs to add to the end of 'Hey, You Down There' explaining what Glar thinks of the situation. Remember that he knows very little about Calvin and Dora, but he has met Calvin briefly. Try to develop Glar's personality. How does he feel about what happened? Do you think he is a successful character? Do you want the reader to laugh or feel a bit scared?

4

1 Adventure

> 1.1 The start of an adventure

The narrative structure of a story is the order in which things happen. This includes how a story starts, when different pieces of information are revealed and how the story ends.

Focus

1 Here is a list of nine events from a story. They are in the wrong order. Rearrange these events into the correct order and then write the new order in the following table. The first one has been done for you.

Events

a Both twins keep their disguises for a month and are unhappy.

b During the journey, a huge storm occurs, and everybody is washed overboard.

c Elizabeth also disguises herself – as an old lady – and arrives at the inn.

d William and Elizabeth are overjoyed to be reunited and return home.

e Elizabeth also swims to the island and she assumes William has not survived.

f Twins William and Elizabeth leave home on a small ship.

g William disguises himself as an old man and gets a job at an inn on the island.

h One day, a huge wind blows, removing their disguises.

i William swims to a nearby island and assumes Elizabeth has not survived.

1 Adventure

	Correct order of events
f	Twins William and Elizabeth leave home on a small ship.

Practice

Most stories are told in chronological order – in the time sequence in which they occur. But some stories use a non-chronological narrative structure. They start with a series of events, then go back in time to explain things that happened earlier.

2 Read the following version of 'Lost at Sea', which is told in non-chronological order. Use different coloured pens to highlight events that occur:

- at the family home
- when the twins are at sea
- on the island.

1.1 The start of an adventure

Lost at Sea

When William and Elizabeth arrived back home, their family were amazed. They couldn't believe it when they walked through the door. William hugged his father and Elizabeth cried as she hugged her mother. They never thought this moment would happen. They could remember swimming through the sea, barely surviving. The ship was destroyed in the storm. They had set off on what they thought was a great adventure across the sea, but as the ship sank, they both lost each other. It was only when that great wind blew off their disguises that they realised the other was alive. William had put on a false beard shortly after he arrived on the island. Elizabeth had also disguised herself. By luck, they had both arrived at the same inn. They were eternally thankful for their good luck as they stood in their parents' house. Being together again was the best feeling ever.

Challenge

3   Look at this list of events. In your notebook, rewrite these events as a story. Use a non-chronological narrative structure. Start by choosing the point you will begin telling the story from.

A Terrible Day
- a   A girl wakes up late – she forgot to set an alarm.
- b   She leaves home but forgets to take her homework and door key.
- c   She runs to school but trips up on the way and hurts her knee.
- d   In her first lesson, she realises she has forgotten her homework.
- e   After school, she walks home alone.
- f   She arrives home but can't find her key.
- g   She sits outside her house. A huge rainstorm soaks her.
- h   She wakes up – she has been having a bad dream.

1 Adventure

> 1.2 Quest!

A monologue is a story or speech given by one character, using the first person voice ('I'). This is different to writing in the third person point of view, which means telling the story from an observer's point of view.

Focus

1 The following sentences from 'Beware Low-Flying Girls' by Katherine Rundell are written in the third person. Rewrite them in the first person.

Odile walked as far as the paths would take her, clapping her hands together in front and behind her back to keep them warm; and then she climbed.

....

....

....

As Odile climbed, she started to feel tired. Her hands struggled to grip the cliff and her eyes started to close.

....

....

....

Suddenly, Odile felt herself falling. She woke with a start and scrambled to grab hold of the rock.

....

....

....

Practice

2   Read the extract from 'Beware Low-Flying Girls', and underline parts of the story or descriptions that you think would appeal to a reader. Make notes on the text to explain your choices.

> Without another word, she pulled on her boots and coat and kissed her grandfather's cheek. He waved her away; <u>his skin was colder than usual</u>.
>
> Odile walked as far as the paths would take her, clapping her hands together in front and behind her back to keep them warm; and then she climbed. It was more of a scramble, really, around the edge of the mountain, but there were places where the ground cut away and dropped to a blur below. She did not fly: the wind might drop at any moment, and she didn't like the idea of so much gravity at once.
>
> The first hint that something was wrong was the smell. Odile sniffed. There were seven layers of scent, none of them good: a between-the-toe smell, a week-old-fish smell, an unbrushed-tooth smell; a **jackdaw**'s breath, a cat's sick pool, a burnt **furball** and a sailor's earwax.
>
> 'Kraiks,' she whispered.
>
> She looked up, up the edge of the mountainside. She could see nothing – only mist, and branches stretching like arms across the rocks. But a voice came down, thin and quiet.
>
> 'Where are you going, little girl?'
>
> Odile said nothing. She set her jaw, and kept climbing, heading sideways.

Helps reader see that grandfather is getting weaker; appeals to reader's feelings of sympathy

jackdaw: a bird (a small crow)
furball: a ball of fur that can develop in an animal's stomach

1 Adventure

Challenge

It is important to present a monologue in an engaging voice.
You can show voice through word choice and the overall tone.

3   Read the last six lines of the extract again. Write a short monologue from the point of view of a Kraik, which is an unpleasant bird-like creature. Use an interesting voice that shows the Kraik's personality.

....

....

....

....

....

....

> 1.3 Train trouble

Language focus

Writers use different types of sentences for different effects. For example, a simple sentence can provide basic, clear detail, but it can also create tension. Compound sentences and complex sentences add detail as well as creating effects, such as conveying excitement. When writing about sentences, try to link your comments about the sentence type to the effect it creates. For example, think about what the shortness of a sentence suggests about the narrator's feelings. Does the detail of a complex sentence help to suggest busyness or panic?

Focus

1   Use different colours to highlight the various sentence types (simple, compound, complex) in the following extract from *Around India in 80 Trains* by Monisha Rajesh.

1.3 Train trouble

> The train had now picked up speed and was racing through the outskirts of Chennai. I looked around. It was a comfort, if not a concern, that after 20 years the trains looked no different. Limp curtains shielded the windows, miniature cockroaches flitted across the seat backs and the fan still blew **ineffectual** wisps of air. A part of me feared that I would board my first train and instantly regret my decision. What if I hated it? Four whole months within these blue walls lay ahead.

ineffectual: useless

Practice

2   Complete the following table by writing in your own examples of different sentence types.

Sentence type	Example
Simple sentence	
Compound sentence	
Complex sentence	

1 Adventure

Challenge

3   In your notebook, write a paragraph that contains different sentence types. Use one of these pictures to inspire you, or write about something from your own imagination.

> 1.4 A hard journey

> **Language focus**
>
> Poets often use different types of sound effects, such as alliteration and sibilance. These sound patterns are effective when the poem is read aloud. They are used sometimes for very specific effects.
>
> Alliteration is when consonant sounds are repeated at the start of words (for example, 'the rifle's rapid rattle' – the repeated 'r' sound brings to mind the stuttering sound of a gun being fired).
>
> Sibilance is the repetition of soft consonant sounds, usually the 's' sound (for example, 'the ship moved slowly through the sea' – the repeated 's' sound brings to mind the sound of a ship moving through water, or the sound of the wind making the ship move).

1.4 A hard journey

Focus

1 Read the two extracts from the poem 'After Apple-Picking' by Robert Frost. It is about a man who has spent the day picking apples and is very tired. Use two colours to highlight examples of sibilance and alliteration.

> Essence of winter sleep is on the night,
> The scent of apples: I am drowsing off.
> I cannot rub the strangeness from my sight
> I got from looking through a pane of glass
> I skimmed this morning from the drinking trough
> And held against the world of **hoary** grass.
> It melted, and I let it fall and break.

hoary: covered in frost

> I feel the ladder sway as the boughs bend.
> And I keep hearing from the cellar bin
> The rumbling sound
> Of load on load of apples coming in.
> For I have had too much
> Of apple-picking: I am overtired
> Of the great harvest I myself desired.
> There were ten thousand thousand fruit to touch,
> Cherish in hand, lift down, and not let fall.
> For all
> That struck the earth,
> No matter if not bruised or spiked with stubble,
> Went surely to the cider-apple heap
> As of no worth.

1 Adventure

Practice

2 What effect is created by the examples you have spotted from 'After Apple-Picking'? Choose one example of sibilance and one of alliteration and make notes on the text to explain the examples.

Challenge

3 Try writing your own sentences using the sound patterns covered in this session. Start with the following ideas:

  a a description of a stormy sea

  ....

  ....

  b the sounds of a battle

  ....

  ....

  c a busy city at night

  ....

  ....

> 1.5 Danger!

Language focus

To create excitement in suspense stories, writers often use verbs that suggest movement and power. In the first paragraph of *Silverfin* by Charlie Higson there are lots of 'action' verbs, including *struggled*, *gripping* and *slid*. These powerful verbs create excitement in the story, helping the reader imagine the movement and danger that the character is experiencing. Verbs build intensity, so choosing a powerful verb like *struggled* is often more effective in creating excitement than the choice of adjective.

Focus

1. Read the following extract from *Silverfin* by Charlie Higson.
   Underline ten interesting and/or powerful verbs.
   One has been done for you.

> Every insane decision he'd taken so far had paid off: going down the branch of the pine tree, <u>swinging</u> on to the wall, climbing down the well shaft, dropping into the pool . . . He had to trust in his own crazy guardian angel.
>
> He let out another bubble of air and pulled himself into the gap, which scraped him on all sides, grazing his spine. But he could still go forward, wriggling like an eel himself, pushing with knees and elbows, crawling with his fingertips along the rock. He was going to make it. He'd made the right choice. He let out the last of his breath and squirmed forward, racing against time, his blood singing in his ears, his head wanting to explode, his lungs full of acid.
>
> And then he stopped.
>
> He could go no further.
>
> What was it?
>
> One of the bundles had got caught behind him. He jerked his hips to try and free it. Come on! Come on! He couldn't get a hand back to untie his belt. He wormed his body backwards to give the bundle some slack, then jerked forward again. He'd done it. He was free. He was moving again.
>
> No. His fingers felt something. Solid rock.
>
> He'd come to a dead end.

1 Adventure

Practice

2 Look at the powerful verbs you underlined in the extract. Choose five of them and suggest replacements for these verbs that have a similar effect. Use a thesaurus to help you.

Verb in text	Replacement
1	
2	
3	
4	
5	

Challenge

3 Write a paragraph describing one of the following scenes. Use interesting and/or powerful verbs that help the reader to picture the scene.

- an out-of-control car heading through a tunnel
- a huge, unexpected storm during a sports game
- a wild animal walking through a busy town.

....

....

....

....

....

....

> 1.6 Creating suspense

Writers use different methods to create suspense. Careful choice of words and phrases can help to create a feeling of danger. The way a story is structured also helps to create suspense.

Focus

1 Read the following story and underline words and phrases that suggest danger.

> I stood on the cliff face and looked down at the furious, boiling waters – I'd dreamt of this moment. The air. The sea. The freedom. My dreams of liberty and closeness to nature had led me here. Further along this cliff face was a place of wonder: it was a cave rumoured to contain strange, beautiful creatures that only a few humans had seen. But to get to the cave, I would need to leap into the ocean then climb up to the cave. This was no easy thing. People had died attempting such a feat – it was madness.
>
> All my life I had avoided danger. But sometimes, life has a strange way of opening your eyes. The ocean looked angry; the ocean was certain death.
>
> The air is so fresh here. There is a comfort in the hypnotic noise of the seabirds, calling you into possible destruction. I breathed deeply, controlling my fear, reminding myself of the reason I was here. Even with my eyes shut, I could see the vivid colours of sea and sky. The sea was beautiful.
>
> This will be a symbolic fall. I may not make it.

Practice

2 Read the following outline of a story. Write a paragraph in which you:
- explain what the main cause of suspense is in the story
- explain the point where the suspense ends.

1 Adventure

Hospital Story

a   A girl and her parents are walking into a hospital.
b   None of the characters speak as they walk down a long corridor.
c   The girl wonders what the doctor will say.
d   They enter the ward and see lots of doctors and nurses gathered around a bed.
e   There is a boy on the bed – it's the girl's brother.
f   The brother isn't moving.
g   A doctor asks to speak to the family in private.
h   The family wait in another room quietly.
i   The doctor enters after 30 minutes.
j   He tells the family that the boy will make a full recovery.

....
....
....
....
....
....
....

Challenge

3   Choose a section from 'Hospital Story' that contains suspense.
    In your notebook, write your own version of this section.
    Use the methods you have learnt to create suspense, including:

  - the right voice
  - sentence types
  - sound patterns
  - word choices.

2 'Hey, You Down There'

> 2.1 Calvin and Dora

> **Language focus**
>
> Writers choose sentence openings carefully to show the reader how events in a story or points in an argument are connected. These connections may relate to:
>
> - **when** (time/sequence of events): for example, 'Later that day . . .' tells the reader that time has moved on in a story
> - **where** (location or context): for example, 'On the other side of the road . . .' indicates a new setting in relation to the previous one
> - **how** (comparison/contrast): for example, 'In the same way . . .' suggests that what comes next is similar to what came before
> - **why** (relationship between events): for example, 'Because of the bad weather . . .' shows a cause, which will be followed by a consequence.

Focus

1   Match these sentence openings to their function. Draw a line between the sentence opening and the correct description of its function in the right-hand column.

Sentence opening	Purpose
On the contrary . . .	To indicate a shift in time
After dinner . . .	To show a change in location
Back at the hotel . . .	To suggest how one event relates to another
As a result . . .	To make a comparison

19

2 'Hey, You Down There'

Practice

2 Read the following extract, taking note of how each sentence begins.

> After half an hour, Rafi Hussein pushed his way to the front of the hot, crowded bus, and stepped into the fresh air. Finding a café in the shopping mall, he settled into a seat in the corner. However, it wasn't a very pleasant place: it was large and empty and a little cold. Above his head, a wasp buzzed around a flickering light. Unexpectedly, a voice rang out.
>
> 'Rafi!' said the voice. It was Asif, his old school friend. Rafi was delighted to meet Asif again. As they sat and talked, Rafi began to remember how much fun they'd had back in their school days.

Complete the table by describing the function of each sentence opening. One has been done for you.

Sentence opening	Purpose
After half an hour . . .	To tell the reader how much time has passed
Finding a café . . .	
However, . . .	
Above his head, . . .	
Unexpectedly, . . .	
As they sat and talked, . . .	

2.1 Calvin and Dora

Challenge

3   Write the first paragraph of a story inspired by the following picture.
    You could introduce a second character, major event or dialogue.
    Choose your sentence openings carefully to help the reader understand
    how events in the story are connected.

....

....

....

....

....

....

....

....

....

2 'Hey, You Down There'

> 2.2 Down the hole

Language focus

Writers use a range of grammatical structures to build information in a story. Sometimes, they use adjectives and adverbs to add detail. Compound-complex sentences can help organise these details. For example:

> As the rope slackened in her hands indicating that the bucket had reached the bottom [1], a scream of sheer terror came up from the hole, and [3] the rope ladder jerked violently [2].

Here, the compound sentence comes second, with the coordinating conjunction joining the two clauses. The subordinate clause comes first and ends with a comma. The sentence is organised this way so the reader pictures the events in the order in which they happen. It shows how one action causes another.

[1] subordinate clause

[2] compound sentence

[3] coordinating conjunction

Focus

1 Put a tick to indicate which of these sentences are compound-complex.

   a   I ran hurriedly into school and then made my way to the classroom, never once pausing for breath. ☐

   b   Tomorrow I am going to buy a new toothbrush and a hairbrush from the pharmacy. ☐

   c   I would like you to come to my birthday party which starts at 6 p.m. on Sunday. ☐

   d   Although I had very little time, I cooked dinner for my family and washed all of the dishes. ☐

Practice

2 Write some of your own compound-complex sentences to express the following ideas:

   a   Two people are in a car. They are late for work.

   ....

   ....

   ....

22

b You are jogging. A dog is chasing you.

....

....

....

c A man watches an old building collapse.

....

....

....

Challenge

Using a range of simple, compound, complex and compound-complex sentences will shape your writing and make it interesting.

3 Write a paragraph about a family celebration. Vary your sentences to create detail and drama. Include at least one compound-complex sentence. Use commas and other punctuation to make sure your meaning is clear.

....

....

....

....

....

....

....

2 'Hey, You Down There'

> 2.3 Gold!

As stories develop, writers give the reader more information about a character. The character's reaction to events reveals more about them. Characters may be seen to change for the better or become less likeable. These changes can alter the reader's impression of them.

Focus

1. Look closely at the way the writer Harold Rolseth describes Calvin's actions in this extract. Highlight key words and phrases that tell you about Calvin's character and attitudes.

> 'Gold,' said Calvin, his voice shaky. 'Must be a whole pound of it . . . and just for a **measly** flashlight. They must be crazy down there.'
>
> He thrust the gold bar into his pocket and opened the small piece of parchment. One side was closely covered with a fine writing. Calvin turned it this way and that and then tossed it on the ground.
>
> 'Foreigners,' he said. 'No wonder they ain't got any sense. But it's plain they need flashlights.'
>
> 'But, Calvin,' said Dora. 'How could they get down there? There ain't any mines in this part of the country.'
>
> 'Ain't you ever heard of them secret government projects?' asked Calvin scornfully. 'This must be one of them. Now I'm going to town to get me a load of flashlights. They must need them bad. Now, mind you watch that hole good. Don't let no one go near it.'

measly: almost worthless

Practice

2. Use the words and phrases you have highlighted to explain how the writer uses language to convey Calvin's character. Start by describing Calvin's manner and attitude, then use examples to show how the words and phrases create this impression. Think about his use of non-standard English. Write about 100 words.

24

....
....
....
....
....
....
....
....
....

Challenge

3   Read the following extract from a story about a character called Ahmed. What impression of this character does the writer create? How have words and phrases helped create that impression? Write a 100-word explanation in your notebook.

> At the end of the day, Ahmed ran out of school as fast as he could. A broad smile danced across his face as he sped over the bridge. Nothing could stop him. His heart raced and the wind tousled his hair. Sunlight caught his features. He'd waited months for this.
>
> Breathlessly, he entered his house. The brother who he hadn't seen for months was standing there, arms open. Ahmed burst into tears of joy.

2 'Hey, You Down There'

> 2.4 Glar the Master

> **Language focus**
>
> Writers choose formal or informal language, depending on their audience and purpose. For example, when writing an email to a friend, or to make conversation sound more realistic in a story, you would use informal language. This might include shorter sentences, contractions and colloquial language. Formal language is used when addressing people you do not know or when discussing more serious topics. Formal writing should sound polite, and should use formal words and grammatically correct sentences.

Focus

1   Which of these two pieces of writing is more formal: A or B? ....

> **A**   As the car sped furiously down the road, I remained absolutely still and a procession of fearsome thoughts cascaded through my brain. What would happen if the driver lost control? Such considerations did not bear thinking about. I quivered and proceeded further down the pavement.

> **B**   As the car went faster down the road, I stood still and loads of bad thoughts went through my head. What happened if the car skidded? I couldn't bear to think. I was shaking but I carried on walking anyhow.

Practice

2   The tone of Glar's letter is formal. The dialogue between Dora and Calvin is much less formal. The narrator's voice is more varied, using a mixture of formal and more straightforward vocabulary. Highlight what you consider to be the formal words in the following extract from 'Hey, You Down There' by Harold Rolseth.

The warm sunlight felt good on her back and it was pleasant to sit and do nothing. She had no fear that Calvin would return soon. She doubted that he would return before morning.

After half an hour Dora gave the line a questioning tug, but it did not yield. She did not mind. It was seldom that she had time to idle away. Usually when Calvin went to town, he burdened her with chores that were to be done during his absence.

Dora waited another half hour before tugging at the line again. This time there was a sharp answering jerk, and Dora began hauling the bucket upward. It seemed much heavier now, and twice she had to pause for a rest. When the bucket reached the surface, she saw why it was heavier.

Dora took the gold bars and buried them in the loose black soil. She paid no heed to the sound of a car coming down the highway at high speed until it passed the house and a wild squawking sounded above the roar of the motor. She hurried around to the front of the house, knowing already what had happened. She stared in dismay at the four chickens which lay dead in the road.

Challenge

3 In your notebook, write two accounts of an event at school. It could be a lesson, a sports event or something that happened at lunchtime. Write one account from the point of view of a learner, using less formal language. Write the second account of the same event from a teacher's point of view, using more formal language. Try to write 100 words for each account.

> 2.5 Back down the hole

Although characters are fictional, writers use them to show themes about human nature. For example, Calvin is used to explore ideas about greed and selfishness. Dora represents a kinder, more thoughtful type of person.

Focus

1 Highlight words and phrases in the following extracts that reveal Dora's character and experiences.

2 'Hey, You Down There'

a She sat down again to enjoy the luxury of doing nothing. When, an hour later, she picked up the line, there was an immediate response from below. The bucket was exceedingly heavy this time, and she was fearful that the line might break.

b 'Fix me something to eat,' he ordered Dora.

Dora hurried into the house and began preparing eggs. Each moment she expected Calvin to come in and demand to know what was holding up his meal.

c 'Your breakfast is ready, Calvin,' said Dora.

'Shut up,' Calvin answered.

d Dora was almost numb with fear. What would happen when the flashlights came back up, with an insulting note in English, was too horrible to contemplate.

Practice

2 In the story, Calvin treats Dora badly. Explore ideas about the theme of power in relationships.

Practise using quotations to support points about theme. Use extracts a–d to write four sentences about the theme of power in the story.

Challenge

3 The theme of power is a common one in stories. In your notebook, write a script that shows how two characters with different amounts of power talk to each other. Your script does not have to include a nasty character like Calvin, but it should show the different ways people speak. The conversation should last one to two minutes when performed.

Start by thinking about the different ways the characters address each other. Do they use first names or titles? Who speaks most? Who asks more questions? Your characters could be:

- a police officer and member of the public
- a doctor and patient
- a sportsperson and referee.

> 2.6 Turkey

Writers take great care to make sure the endings of stories satisfy readers. It can be exciting to add a twist to the tale as a surprise, but readers should never feel let down by the ending of a story.

Focus

1 Read this story outline. Explain briefly what you think happens at the end of the story.

> **The Missing Child**
>
> A powerful ruler has a young child – the child goes missing. Nobody knows where she has gone. The ruler is very upset. He employs a local warrior to find her. The warrior discovers that the daughter has been kidnapped and sets out to to find her. After weeks of travelling, he discovers the daughter and confronts the kidnappers.

....

....

....

2 'Hey, You Down There'

Practice

At the end of a story, a writer usually shows how characters have been rewarded or punished for their actions. They may fall in love, find something or develop as a person. Sad stories may end with people falling out of love or sometimes even dying. However, in some stories, the writer may not reveal what happens to a character – they will leave the ending open.

2 Complete the table showing what each character learns or experiences at the end of 'Hey, You Down There'. Consider these questions:

- Is there a sad or happy ending for the character?
- Have they changed or learnt anything new?
- Are they rewarded or punished?
- Are there any characters whose ending is left open?

Calvin:
Dora:
Glar:

Challenge

3 In your notebook, write two paragraphs to add to the end of 'Hey, You Down There' explaining what Glar thinks of the situation. Remember that he knows very little about Calvin and Dora, but he has met Calvin briefly. Try to develop Glar's personality. How does he feel about what happened? Do you think he is a successful character? Do you want the reader to laugh or feel a bit scared?

3 Film and fame

> 3.1 Meeting your hero

> **Language focus**
>
> When using direct speech in fiction, you can use some features of spoken English to make dialogue seem realistic. For example, using contractions such as 'I've' instead of 'I have' can sound more like speech. Make sure you follow the rules of punctuating dialogue:
> - Put a new speaker on a new line.
> - Put the words spoken by a character inside speech marks.
> - Start each new sentence of dialogue with a capital letter.
> - Use punctuation accurately inside speech marks.

Focus

1   Read these sentences of dialogue. Write out the underlined words as contractions, using an apostrophe.

'<u>It is</u> very unfair that I always get blamed.' ....

'She <u>could not</u> eat it.' ....

'<u>She had</u> seen me hiding.' ....

'It <u>was not</u> me.' ....

'I <u>did not</u> notice the fly in my dinner.' ....

3 Film and fame

Practice

2 This text contains dialogue, but it has not been correctly set out. Read the text, then:

- use a highlighter to identify any contraction or dialogue errors
- rewrite the text on the lines using the correct punctuation.

> Hassan and Amir were really looking forward to the preview of the new *Star Wars* film. 'ive been told that its great' said Amir. 'me too' said Hassan. 'its meant to be quite modern in its outlook' said Amir. 'what do you mean' said Hassan. 'i mean its got a much stronger role for the lead female'. Good said Hassan I couldnt bear it if the strong characters were only male or strange monsters. 'what time does it start' asked Amir. In one hour said Hassan. Lets set off now said Amir.

....

....

....

....

....

....

....

....

....

....

Challenge

3   Write a dialogue between two people. Use contractions and make sure that speech is set out and punctuated accurately. You could use an idea of your own or choose one of the following situations:

- a pair of friends talking about music
- a teacher and a learner talking at the end of a lesson
- a son and father talking about birthdays
- two girls talking about a sports game.

3 Film and fame

> 3.2 Predicting the story

> **Language focus**
>
> Nouns are a key part of any description. Proper nouns are used for specific places and people, like 'Shanghai' or 'William'. Concrete nouns give the reader an idea of 'real' objects in a scene, such as 'table', 'cat', 'guitar'. Abstract nouns help to convey feelings and ideas, such as 'love' or 'freedom'.
>
> Writers use adjectives to tell you more about a noun. Adjectives can give detail about size, appearance or manner, for example, 'large', 'beautiful', 'angry'. Adjective–noun combinations provide readers with a quick image of a situation, person or thing, for example, 'freezing rain' or 'large horse'.

Focus

1 Read the definitions of types of nouns.

Noun type	Definition	Example
Concrete noun	Something you can see or touch.	sock, car, apple
Abstract noun	Something you cannot touch, such as ideas or feelings.	anger, the past
Proper noun	Names of people and places, special holidays, the titles of books, plays or films, or a time. Proper nouns begin with a capital letter.	Indra, Mumbai, *Godzilla*

a Write a sentence that contains a concrete noun.

....

....

b Write a sentence that contains an abstract noun.

....

....

c Write a sentence that contains a proper noun.

....

....

Practice

To write an effective story, a writer needs to describe a setting in a way that helps the reader imagine the scene. Later in *Film Boy*, Prem visits the home of the actor. He is a rich man who lives a life of luxury. The following extract describes the setting of the actor's home.

> A tiger's head with fixed, glaring eyes was mounted on one wall, and on another there was the stuffed head of an antelope.
>
> Quietly he moved through the hall and into the room beyond. This was a living room, a room which stretched out in all directions. At one end there was a large piano topped with vases of flowers, at another end there were sofas and chairs covered with zebra skin. In the middle of the room there was a marble floor in the shape of a giant star, with each point a different colour.
>
> Prem stood in silent wonderment. He had seen rooms like this in films, but he had never imagined that there would be such places right here in Bombay.

2 Select three examples of adjective–noun combinations from the extract and explain what image is created by them. Think about how the words help you to imagine and understand the room.

Example 1: ....

....

....

Example 2: ....

....

....

Example 3: ....

....

....

3 Film and fame

Challenge

3 Write a paragraph describing your own room or home. Use proper and common nouns to focus on details that reveal something about yourself, your family, your values or your culture. Use the ideas from *Film Boy* as a model. You should choose adjectives carefully to show details about size, colour and appearance. Remember to use standard English.

....

....

....

....

....

....

....

....

....

....

> 3.3 Real lives, real problems

Newspaper headlines are used to sell newspapers. For serious articles, they can be factual and informative. Newspapers that are more focused on entertainment and gossip use a variety of eye-catching techniques to interest readers and encourage them to buy the paper.

3.3 Real lives, real problems

Focus

1 Look at this list of language features found in newspaper articles. Draw a line to join the feature with the correct definition.

Feature	Definition
alliteration	three dots that show that a statement is unfinished or has text missing, to create suspense or encourage the reader to finish the sentence
pun	! to express surprise or excitement
rhetorical question	a question that does not expect an answer
ellipses	two or more words that have the same sound
exaggeration	using the same first letter for several words
rhyme	to present something as worse or better than it is
informal language	words and phrases that are relaxed and less serious
exclamation mark	a joke using a single word that has more than one meaning

Practice

2 Look at these headlines. Which of the techniques listed in Activity 1 are used here? Write the technique next to the headline. You may be able to see more than one technique in a headline.

a **NOT AT ALL FARE!** ....

b **A shoal lot of fun…** ....

c **Weird and wonderful Whales!** ....

d **THE END OF THE MALE RACE AS WE KNOW IT?** ....

3 Film and fame

e Violence rife on our streets... ....

f LITERACY LEVELS LOWEST EVER IN OUR CITIES! ....

Challenge

3   Here are three summaries of newspaper articles. For each one, write a headline then annotate it to show the technique(s) you have used. Refer to the listing in the Focus section if needed.

A 14-year-old chess champion from your country has beaten the current world adult champion.

Headline: ....

....

....

Researchers have developed a new miracle glue that can heal wounds in seconds.

Headline: ....

....

....

A new planet larger than Earth but smaller than Neptune has been discovered.

Headline: ....

....

....

> 3.4 Reviewing films

Film reviews contain a number of typical features. The use of some of these features depends on the type of film and its intended audience. For instance, a review of a serious film for adults might give information about the director's other films.

Focus

1   Look at this list. Some features are only likely to appear in reviews of serious films for adults. However, some other features are likely to appear in reviews of both serious and family films. Put a tick in the column you think is more appropriate.

		Serious film	Both serious and family films
1	Title of the film		
2	Reviewer's/journalist's name		
3	Comments about camera shots		
4	Actors' names		
5	Details about other films		
6	Information about the production company		
7	The stories of other films the actors have starred in		
8	Positive or negative language to convey judgement		
9	Comments on different edits or versions of the film		
10	Details about the plot		

Which features were more difficult to decide on and why?

……

……

……

……

3 Film and fame

Practice

2   Read this film review. It is about a film aimed at teenagers and young adults. On the review, label any features you can find from the list in Activity 1.

> ### *Car Trouble*: a film with no fuel in the tank
> ### By Ali Ling
>
> *Car Trouble* is the final film in a sequence of three films directed by Emil Smith. Those of you who watched the previous film – *Going Nowhere Fast* – might be a bit disappointed with this one. It's not the best.
>
> The film, set in 1950s America, starts with a fast car chase, at the end of which a big crash occurs. Fortunately, no one is seriously hurt. Emerging from the wreckage is Sam Priest, the main character who is played by Jonny Jonsson. The story then goes back in time to explain how the car chase happened. Priest's wife, Melissa (played by Kim Stone), had been kidnapped by Priest's business rival. After a ransom demand and some detective work, Priest catches up with the kidnappers, leading to the car chase. This is probably the best part of the film. The second half is much less exciting. It focuses on the family life of Sam and Melissa Priest, and although it's well acted, nothing much happens.
>
> This final film of three will disappoint many fans. It's a particular shame for Jonny Jonsson, an actor with so much talent. My advice would be to wait until his new film, *A New Tomorrow*, comes out at the end of the month. Early reviews suggest it is excellent.

Challenge

3 Decide whether the language suggests the review is giving a positive or negative judgement. Write your answer and explain your reasons with examples.

....

....

....

....

....

....

....

> 3.5 Writing a review

Films are categorised according to genre, just like books. This gives viewers an idea about what they are going to watch.

Focus

1 These extracts are bits of dialogue taken from different types of films. Next to each one, write a letter showing which genre of film they represent.

3 Film and fame

Use the following key:

| W = war story | F = fantasy |
| L = love/romance | S = science fiction |

a 'Things don't always work out the way they should, but we were meant for each other.' ....

b 'We will use the proton-mediator. In that way, we will split time and space.' ....

c 'Each and every man under my command owes this to his country. We are in this together.' ....

d 'Ronmea, I will take the ring to the planet of Armor, though the journey is far.' ....

Practice

Most reviews include both positive and negative statements. In Activity 1, notice how connectives such as 'but' and 'though' are used to organise the sentences and suggest a contrast:

- *'Things don't always work out the way they should, <u>but</u> we were meant for each other.'*
- *'Ronmea, I will take the ring to the planet of Armor, <u>though</u> the journey is far.'*

2 Practise structuring your sentences to express contrasting views, as in Activity 1. You could write about the acting, plot, music, ending, etc. Write three sentences using some of these words and phrases.

- little to recommend it
- disappointing
- worth seeing
- high points
- a hard-hitting message
- a skilled piece of filmmaking
- must not be missed
- a predictable storyline
- an unsatisfying ending
- definitely worth missing
- a moving portrayal

3.5 Writing a review

Challenge

3   Write the opening paragraph of a review text on a film from your own imagination. You should:

- give the film a name and the review a title
- establish the genre of the film
- give a brief overview of the plot
- include a sentence which contains a positive and negative statement.

3 Film and fame

> 3.6 Preparing a speech

Writing and delivering a persuasive speech means thinking carefully about the content and phrasing of your speech.

Focus

1   Persuasive speeches contain facts and opinions. Look at these statements, which are about the famous Jamaican nurse Mary Seacole. Which do you think are facts and which sound like opinion? Place a tick in the correct column.

Statement	Fact	Opinion
Mary was the best nurse in the world.		
She received four medals from the British government.		
I think Mary deserved to be treated fairly.		
Mary's mother taught her to use traditional medicines.		
Mary was born in 1805.		
Jamaican medicine is the most effective medicine.		
Mary volunteered as a nurse during the Crimean War.		
She was not allowed to help during the war.		
Everyone knows and loves Mary Seacole.		
Mary died in 1881.		

Practice

2   Which famous person would you choose to visit your class?
    Note down which characteristics you admire in your chosen celebrity.

    Read this speech, in which a learner argues that they would choose Emma Watson to visit the class. Then complete the activities that follow.

> The person I would choose to visit our class is the actor, Emma Watson. She is a fantastic actor who played Hermione in the Harry Potter films. Perhaps I am combining the two characters in my mind! Hermione can be admired because she is hard-working and clever. I would guess that Emma Watson must have also worked hard to have achieved so much so young.

3.6 Preparing a speech

Emma was born in 1990 and appeared in the first Harry Potter film in 2001. When most of her friends would have been in school studying, she was acting. She still managed to get a university degree from Oxford. She has continued to be a public figure after her early films. She is famous for arguing for equality between men and women. She helped launch the UN Women campaign 'HeForShe'. The campaign encourages men to support equality between men and women. Her experiences make her a very interesting person. I think she is an excellent role model to introduce to the class.

a Write a list of five facts about Emma Watson from the speech.

....

....

....

....

....

b Write down five words that give an opinion about Emma Watson.

....

....

....

....

....

c Which sentences do you find most persuasive and why? Underline two sentences and explain why you think they are persuasive.

....

....

....

3 Film and fame

....

....

....

Challenge

Varying sentence lengths and types can add rhythm and interest to a speech.
For example, in the first paragraph of the Emma Watson speech, the learner writes:

Hermione can be admired because she is hard-working and clever. I would guess that Emma Watson must have also worked hard to have achieved so much so young.

These sentences could be rewritten like this:

Why do people admire Hermione? It's for two reasons, I think. One — she's hard-working and two — she's clever. Is Emma Watson like Hermione? I guess she must be to have achieved so much so young.

3   Rewrite the second paragraph from the speech.
    Vary the sentence types and length to add rhythm and interest.

....

....

....

....

....

....

....

....

4 Small but perfect

> 4.1 Flash fiction

> **Language focus**
>
> In literature, a symbol is an object or sign that represents something else. These signs can be seen in everyday life, from music to chemistry, from street signs to food packaging. Some are universally understood, but some are particular to specific countries. For example, in many countries, schoolchildren understand that the cross sign – 'x' – can symbolise something wrong or incorrect.

Focus

1   Look at these images. What do you understand by these signs?

……………………………………………………………………
……………………………………………………………………
……………………………………………………………………
……………………………………………………………………

……………………………………………………………………
……………………………………………………………………
……………………………………………………………………
……………………………………………………………………

4 Small but perfect

Practice

People may interpret symbols in different ways, depending on the context. For example, in some contexts, the colour red might symbolise danger. In others, it could symbolise love. A white flag could be seen as a positive symbol representing peace or as a sign of surrender – a sign of weakness.

2 Consider the following items used as symbols. What qualities do they represent? What situations and people do you associate with them? Are they positive or negative?

    a   a gold medal

....

....

....

    b   a snake

....

....

....

    c   an apple

....

....

....

Challenge

Read the short story 'Seeds'.

> I loved my grandfather. He was always around when I was growing up. I think he worked in a factory, but as long as I'd known him, he was retired. He loved gardens and plants. He had a greenhouse and used to grow vegetables and flowers. I remember playing in his beautiful garden when I was growing up. He used to bring flowers for my mother once a week.

As he got older, he couldn't look after the garden as well. I tried, but by that point in my life, I had a full-time job and couldn't spare much time. It was really sad to see the garden overgrown. The plants were dying and the weeds grew instead.

When we knew that my grandfather didn't have long left to live, we spent more time together. One day, at his bedside, he gave me a packet of seeds and told me to plant them. That was the last time I saw him. I was really upset. In the weeks after, I planted the seeds and to be honest, forgot about them.

Then one day in late winter, I looked out of my window and saw that flowers were growing. Snowdrops. Beautiful, delicate white flowers. Snowdrops are tough flowers – they come out in cold weather. I smiled and for a moment, the sun came out.

3 There are several natural references in the story (the garden, seeds and snowdrops). These could be read as symbols. Using your own words, summarise what they might symbolise.

....

....

....

....

....

....

....

....

....

4 Small but perfect

> 4.2 Small but precious

> **Language focus**
>
> Writers often tell stories that stretch over a period of time. For example, a narrator might start by explaining what happened 50 years ago, then move to another time period, before finally explaining how they feel about things 'now'. Time connectives such as 'then', 'next', 'before', 'after some time' or 'years later' are sometimes used to support the reader's understanding of the sequence of events and how they are linked.

Focus

1. Reread the story 'Seeds' in Session 4.1. Highlight the time connectives.

Practice

Some stories are told in a chronological sequence – this is the order in which events happen. Other stories 'move around' more and put events in a different time sequence to the order in which they happened.

2. Read the text below and highlight the time connectives.

> **Chance Meeting**
>
> In March 2015, I was sitting in a café, reading my book and enjoying my lunch break. Five years earlier, when I started this job, I found this café and had been going there ever since. The first day at my job was tough. I remember feeling lonely and unsure what to do. The office was huge. Then, at lunchtime, I walked into town and found this lovely little café. It was a real pleasure to have some time to sit and relax.
>
> So, as I sat in the café, I finished my book and gazed out of the window and I saw somebody I hadn't seen for a long time. Karen. Years ago, she was my best friend at school. We had fallen out and lost touch. The next day, the same thing happened. There was Karen, walking past, dressed for work and looking stylish. I got up and caught up with her.
>
> Now, three years later, we are very good friends. I'm meeting her for lunch in a minute at my favourite café.

The story moves around between time periods. Write down what happens in the story in date order.

At school:

....

....

....

2010:

....

....

....

March 2015:

....

....

....

2018:

....

....

....

Challenge

3   In your notebook, write a short story that is told in a different order.
    Use time connectives to help the reader understand the sequence.
    Write 150–200 words.

4 Small but perfect

> 4.3 Haiku poetry

The Japanese poetic form haiku consists of three lines. Typically, the first and third lines contain five syllables and the second line contains seven syllables. It often concentrates on one main idea or image, but sometimes it links two ideas together.

Focus

1. Which of these three versions of a haiku poem do not follow the typical pattern of syllables?

   ....

   A

   Falling like stars

   The autumn leaves drop to the ground

   The summer is over.

   B

   Falling like a star

   The first autumn leaf drops drown

   The summer is over.

   C

   Falling like a star

   The first autumn leaf drops drown

   Summer is over.

4.3 Haiku poetry

Practice

2 Read through this extended haiku poem, 'Tube Strike Haiku', by Roger McGough. It is about a day in London when the underground trains were not running.

> trains that are side-lined
> **idling** in rusty sidings
> fear the **knacker's yard**
> * * *
> tunnels empty now
> can see the light at both ends
> birds risk a short cut
> * * *
> rails sleeping, dream of
> a parallel universe
> a new perspective
> * * *
> platforms yawn and stretch
> enjoying the holiday
> mice minding the gap

idling: doing nothing
knacker's yard: a place where old or injured animals are taken to be killed once they are no longer useful

a How many syllables does the title have?

....

b Do all the verses follow the syllable rules of haiku?

....

c Do you think this poem is a positive or negative poem? Explain your answer.

....

....

4 Small but perfect

Challenge

3   Think of a place that changes when normal activity stops. For example, a school, a supermarket or your home when everyone is out.

   In your notebook, write your own haiku series using the poem 'Tube Strike Haiku' as a model.

> 4.4 Writing imagist poetry

Imagist poems focus on details and visual ideas to create a picture in the reader's mind.

Focus

1   Look closely at this image from nature. Write down a list of what you see.

   ....
   ....
   ....
   ....
   ....
   ....

Practice

2   How could you turn your notes from Activity 1 into an imagist poem? Use the questions to help you plan.

   a   What feeling or idea do you want to convey (for example, peacefulness, danger, beauty)?

       ....

b Select four things you listed in Activity 1 and then extend them into lines of verse.

....

....

....

....

....

....

....

....

c Suggest a suitable title for the poem you have just written.

....

Challenge

3   William Carlos Williams's poem 'The Red Wheelbarrow', in Session 4.4 of the Learner's Book, presents a moment in time. Think about a moment when time seems to stand still. Examples might include:

- a moment in your memory
- a moment in nature such as just before a storm or just after heavy rain
- a moment of crisis or shock
- a picture of your choice which reflects this idea.

Write your own imagist poem which captures that moment.

....

....

4 Small but perfect

....

....

....

....

....

....

....

> 4.5 Miniature art

> **Language focus**
>
> Prefixes perform different functions in English and can change meanings to varying degrees. For example, the prefix 'sub-' suggests something below. For instance, when 'sub-' is added to 'heading' in 'subheading', it refers to a heading beneath another heading. The subheading covers a smaller section of the piece of writing. Other prefixes reverse the meaning of the root word. For example, if you add 'ab-' to 'normal' to create 'abnormal', then the original meaning is reversed. Be careful not to confuse prefixed words with words that look like they have prefixes. For instance, the word 'subject' only exists in English as a word meaning 'topic'.

Focus

1   Look at the list of words. Some contain no prefix at all, some have a prefix and some have one that reverses the meaning of the root word. Complete the chart by placing a tick in the appropriate boxes.

Word	No prefix	Prefix	Prefix that reverses the meaning
dislike			
repaint			
describe			
undertone			
antifreeze			
counterargument			
unwind			
missing			
inaccurate			

Practice

2   Here are five pairs of words. The second of the pair has a prefix that reverses the meaning. Write a sentence containing each word.

   a   correct / incorrect

   ....

   ....

   b   understand / misunderstand

   ....

   ....

   c   agree / disagree

   ....

   ....

   d   possible / impossible

   ....

   ....

4 Small but perfect

Challenge

3   Read the following passage. In it, there are two prefixed words that reverse the meaning of the root word. Highlight these words.

> **Me and My Scooter**
>
> When I was young, I never rode a scooter. This probably sounds strange, but I had no interest at all in them. I didn't like scooters, bikes or any type of sport to be honest. There was also another reason though – my family couldn't afford one. Unlike my privileged friends, I never had the opportunity.
>
> When I grew up and became a mother, I bought my six-year-old son a scooter. In fact, I bought one for the whole family, myself included. I found that I loved it, even though I must look silly, a 40-year-old woman whizzing along the street on a scooter. The neighbours either ignore me, laugh at me or give disapproving looks. It doesn't matter to me. It's great!

> 4.6 Perfect pastimes

Conducting an interview to find information requires careful planning, questioning and listening.

Focus

1   Imagine you are going to interview a person about their job as a writer of young adult fiction, to learn about their work and find out if it is something that you could do yourself in the future.

Look at these questions prepared by another learner. Which ones will help you get the information you need? Tick the five most useful questions.

- When did you first become interested in writing? ☐
- Tell me about your family. ☐
- Were you good at writing when you were at school? ☐
- Can you explain how you first went about deciding to become a full-time writer? ☐

4.6 Perfect pastimes

- Can you explain your routine for writing and a normal workday pattern for you? ☐
- In your opinion, what are the advantages and disadvantages of your work? ☐
- Do you enjoy writing? ☐
- Which is the book that you most enjoyed writing? ☐
- Can you describe how you go about writing – do you plan it or just begin writing? ☐
- Do you use a computer or pen to do your writing? ☐

Practice

2 Here is an excerpt from an interview with a rock musician, Hans Meier, and also the journalist's article based on the excerpt. Look at how the journalist has ordered the information. Use different colours to highlight information in the interview and the corresponding lines in the article.

Interview

INTERVIEWER: What is it that you love about music?

HANS: What a big question! Music means everything to me. There's nothing better than standing on stage playing the music I love to our fans. But I suppose I always loved music from an early age. I can remember listening to the music my parents played at home and being fascinated by the guitar sounds. Whenever I felt unhappy, music changed my mood for the better.

Article

Meier always loved music. As he sat in his leather chair, he thought back to his childhood, explaining how he was 'fascinated by the guitar sounds' in his parents' record collection. It is clear he loves music. He looked almost tearful as he described how it cheered him up when he was down. As an adult though, it's the thrill of playing live to his fans which inspires Hans Meier.

4 Small but perfect

Challenge

3 Now read another excerpt from the interview with Hans Meier. Rewrite it as an article.

> **INTERVIEWER:** Tell me about songwriting.
>
> **HANS:** Well until I was 25, I never wrote songs. It was always other band members who wrote songs.
>
> **INTERVIEWER:** Surely you must have written guitar solos and riffs?
>
> **HANS:** Yes, I did that from as soon as I learnt how to play. But I never wrote lyrics or tunes to sing. In fact, the first time I wrote a song, it was almost by accident. We were recording our first album and we needed a final song. I just happened to be messing about in the studio and the song 'Lost in You' seemed to flow out of me. It became a single and sold a million copies.

....

....

....

....

....

....

....

....

....

5 Unusual education

> 5.1 Unusual schools

> **Language focus**
>
> In explanatory writing, writers use connectives to clarify links between pieces of information. Connectives can be used for comparison, sequencing or qualifying. For example:
>
> Comparison: *I played football for my local team **in the same way** that my father did.*
>
> Sequencing: *Put the pasta in the pan **after** the water has boiled.*
>
> Qualifying: *I didn't buy the coat **because** it didn't fit properly.*
>
> Connectives can also be used to:
> - introduce examples (for example, 'such as')
> - to add ideas (for example, 'furthermore')
> - to summarise (for example, 'on the whole').

Focus

1 Highlight the connectives in this text.

> Just like my sister had three years earlier, I arrived at my new school. I was looking forward to it. My sister said it was a great place to study. Several months earlier, I had visited my new school. I remember that day well. First of all, we met the headteacher and were told about the history of the school. Afterwards, we looked around the building. This made me feel secure, because once I knew what the inside of the school looked like, I began to feel less nervous: I could picture myself there. At the end of the day, I returned home and my parents asked me all about it. I told them I'd love my new school just as much as my old one.

5 Unusual education

Practice

2   Complete the table to identify the purpose of the connectives in each sentence.
    Are they used to:

    • introduce examples?
    • present a sequence?
    • qualify?
    • compare?

Sentence	Purpose
Once I had bought a guitar, I practised every day.	
Amina bought a new bike because the old one was too small.	
There are many fuels (for example, coal, gas and oil).	
After we got married, we moved into our new home.	
I bought a computer even though I couldn't really afford it.	
Chen wanted to be a chef, just like his uncle.	

Challenge

3   In your notebook, write a paragraph for each of the following tasks.
    Choose connectives carefully, selecting the right connective for the purpose.

    a   an explanation of how to get from your house to your school
    b   a piece of persuasive writing arguing that education is the most important part of a young person's life
    c   the opening of a story in which a man is running away.

> 5.2 School uniform

In some texts, bias is obvious. In others, it is harder to spot. Think carefully about the way a writer presents a topic. The phrases a writer uses to describe the topic can help you to identify bias.

Focus

1 Look at these five opinions about school uniform. Which of them are *for* learners wearing school uniform and which are *against*? Place a tick in the correct column.

Opinion	For	Against
a Uniforms make all learners look professional and intelligent.		
b I feel really anonymous in my awful school clothes.		
c Our school uniform makes every learner feel like a robot.		
d I wear my uniform with pride: it's an honour.		
e Every learner loves to wear their school uniform.		

Practice

2 Read this blog, written by a learner at a school that has just introduced a new uniform. Use two different colours to highlight phrases that are:

- informative and neutral – they show no bias
- biased – they present an opinion or give an impression that is unfair.

> This year we have a new school uniform. We were forced to wear it. It was like being in prison. To be fair, the uniform is not expensive compared to the old one. It's also a sensible colour – blue. But the jacket looks like it has been made by a child. The sleeves are 1 km long and the trousers are the worst trousers I've ever seen. It was designed by one of the learners apparently.

5 Unusual education

Challenge

3 In your notebook, write two accounts that give different versions of an event. Keep the informative details the same but include sentences that show an obvious exaggeration or bias. You could start by imagining two different types of people and how they might describe their experiences. Use one of the following ideas, or come up with one of your own.

- A holiday to Europe: one account focuses on occasional bad weather, poor food and boring places to visit. The other account is far more positive.
- A family celebration: one account makes it seem exciting and memorable, the other account suggests it was dull and unhappy.
- A film: one account suggests the film was the best ever, the other account makes the actors and plot seem very poor.

> 5.3 Homeschooling

When reading a text that presents a point of view, it is important to be able to identify and understand the details. You need to read every phrase carefully and think about what the writer means.

Focus

1 Read the following sentences carefully. On the line after each statement, write whether it is a positive experience, a negative one or both positive and negative.

a *Homeschooling can be a difficult experience, but with the right approach, it can also be effective.*

    ....

b *I was homeschooled. It was ineffective and left me unprepared for later life.*

    ....

c *I homeschooled all three of my children. They loved it.*

    ....

5.3 Homeschooling

Practice

Read the following paragraph carefully. It suggests that homeschooling is a positive experience.

> Parents who decide to educate their child at home make great sacrifices. They often give up their own careers and spend their own money buying books and equipment. These parents are often very caring. They put their children's needs firmly ahead of their own. Instead of working or enjoying free time during the day, they spend hours helping their child learn.
>
> Who knows a child best of all? The parents, of course. This means that they can help their child emotionally as well as educationally. They can decide when it's time to work really hard and when it's time to release the pressure on their child. For families, homeschooling is the answer to the question of how to learn best.

2 In your own words, explain what the following sentences mean:

   a *Parents who decide to educate their child at home make great sacrifices.*

      ....

      ....

   b *They put their children's needs firmly ahead of their own.*

      ....

      ....

   c *they can help their child emotionally as well as educationally*

      ....

      ....

   d *release the pressure on their child*

      ....

      ....

5 Unusual education

Challenge

3   Read Farouk's views. In your own words, explain the points he makes in this paragraph about the disadvantages of homeschooling.

> Looking back, I have realised that school prepares you for the rest of your life. School gives you a purpose and routine which prepares you for work. By the time I was 16, I had no qualifications or skills. If I had attended school, I would have found my adult life much easier. I blame homeschooling for a lot of my problems and even now, I can see no reason for me not to have attended school like everyone else.

....

....

....

....

> 5.4 A new challenge

If you fully understand the basic plot and characters in a text, you will start to see how they link together to suggest the bigger ideas and themes the writer is exploring. You also need to 'read beyond the text', thinking carefully about what the writer is suggesting.

Focus

1   Answer these questions about the basic plot points in the extract from *Wonder* by R. J. Palacio.

Extract 1

Next week I start fifth grade. Since I've never been to a real school before, I am pretty much totally and completely petrified. People think I haven't

5.4 A new challenge

gone to school because of the way I look, but it's not that. It's because of all the surgeries I've had. Twenty-seven since I was born. The bigger ones happened before I was even four years old, so I don't remember those. But I've had two or three surgeries every year since then (some big, some small), and because I'm little for my age, and I have some other medical mysteries that doctors never really figured out, I used to get sick a lot. That's why my parents decided it was better if I didn't go to school.

a How many surgeries has Auggie had?

....

....

b What reasons can you find for Auggie not attending school?

....

....

Practice

2 In your own words, explain what the writer implies about Auggie's experiences in these lines:

a *they've always known me the way I am, they're used to me*

....

....

....

b *Zack and Alex always invited me to their birthday parties when we were little, but Joel and Eamonn and Gabe never did.*

....

....

....

5 Unusual education

   c   *Maybe I'm making too big a deal about birthday parties.*

   ....

   ....

   ....

Challenge

3 Read Auggie's account of school and friendships in the next extract from *Wonder*. Write a paragraph to explain what the writer states *explicitly* about feelings about school, and what is *implied* about his friendships.

> ### Extract 2
>
> I can't say I always wanted to go to school because that wouldn't be exactly true. What I wanted was to go to school, but only if I could be like every other kid going to school. Have lots of friends and hang out after school and stuff like that.
>
> I have a few really good friends now. Christopher is my best friend, followed by Zachary and Alex. We've known each other since we were babies. And since they've always known me the way I am, they're used to me. When we were little, we used to have playdates all the time, but then Christopher moved to Bridgeport in Connecticut. That's more than an hour away from where I live in North River Heights, which is at the top tip of Manhattan. And Zachary and Alex started going to school. It's funny: even though Christopher's the one who moved far away, I still see him more than I see Zachary and Alex. They have all these new friends now. If we bump into each other on the street, they're still nice to me, though. They always say hello.
>
> I have other friends, too, but not as good as Christopher and Zack and Alex were. For instance, Zack and Alex always invited me to their birthday parties when we were little, but Joel and Eamonn and Gabe never did. Emma invited me once, but I haven't seen her in a long time. And, of course, I always go to Christopher's birthday. Maybe I'm making too big a deal about birthday parties.

....

....

....
....
....
....
....
....
....

> 5.5 Precepts

Language focus

There are several reasons to use a colon:

- to introduce a list – for example, 'I have three favourite hobbies: reading, tennis and playing the violin.'
- to separate two clauses where the second one explains the first – for example, 'I didn't reply to Nisha's party invitation: I hadn't received it.'
- to emphasise a word or phrase for effect – for example, 'There was only one way out: jump!'

Focus

1 Draw a line to connect each example of how colons are used in the correct way.

The verdict was a foregone conclusion: guilty.	to introduce a list
I packed carefully for Malaysia: sandals, a map, a sunhat and my passport.	to separate two clauses where the second one explains the first
The research on holidays is clear: holidays makes people happy.	to emphasise a word or phrase for effect

5 Unusual education

Practice

2 Read this text. It contains both correct and incorrect uses of colons.
Use two different coloured pens to highlight sentences that contain colons used correctly and those sentences that contain misused colons.

> **The Best Day of My Life**
>
> When I was young, I thought the best day of my life would be when I got a well-paid job: it seemed that that's what life was about. I left school: with high hopes. I had studied hard and loved the following lessons: English, music and art. The very first job I got after school was tough: first jobs always are. It was working in a shop. The shop sold stationery: pens, pencils and card. The hours were: long.
>
> I learnt a lot from my second boss: in the early part of any career, it's essential to have a mentor. He explained that success can come in many forms, for instance: happiness, wealth and relationships. It was a lesson I never forgot: money isn't everything.
>
> As I got older and more experienced: I realised that I would make a good boss. I knew that I should return to college to help me achieve: this. I did some more studying: knowledge is important in the sector I was working in. My time at college required three things: dedication, time and an awful lot of reading!
>
> Although I did become a good boss with a well-paid job, I soon realised a very great truth: family life was far more important. I know this because of one very significant event: the birth of my child. It was the best day of my life by far.

Challenge

3 In your notebook, write a paragraph for one of these three tasks.
Make sure you use colons accurately.

- A simple recipe for a favourite meal.
- An account of why it is important to work hard at school.
- An explanation of what you hope to do in the future and why.

> 5.6 *The Last Class*

Drama scripts convey information in two main ways: through dialogue and stage directions. The audience only hears dialogue – the stage directions are for the benefit of performers and those who are reading the play rather than watching it. However, both these features give key information about characters and events.

Focus

1 Extract 1 reveals a lot about setting and situation.
   Tick the statements that you are definitely true.

> **Extract 1**
>
> *Morning. A street with heavy rain. Two schoolgirls are walking quickly.*
>
> SISI: *(angrily)* I can't believe this! First day back at school and it's pouring down. My hair will be ruined!
>
> CHEN: And we're in Mr Ling's class. He's meant to be really old – and strict.
>
> SISI: Really? That's not what my brother said.
>
> CHEN: What do you mean?
>
> SISI: My brother said he was . . . brilliant . . . in a strange way.
>
> CHEN: Really? Cool.

Statement	True?
The weather is not very good.	
Chen is angry.	
Sisi is angry.	
The girls have a new teacher.	
Chen's sister was in Mr Ling's class.	
Sisi's brother was in Mr Ling's class.	
Sisi can't quite explain Mr Ling's personality.	

5 Unusual education

Practice

2 Explain, in your own words, what you learn about Chen in the conversation in Extract 2.

....

....

....

....

> **Extract 2**
>
> SISI: I'm just about dry now. What should we do after school?
>
> CHEN: I don't know. Don't you wish that something exciting would happen, just once?
>
> SISI: Like what?
>
> CHEN: I don't know. Something different. Something unexpected.

3 Describe the relationship between Mr Ling and Mrs Zhou in Extract 3. Think about who seems most powerful and how that is shown in the dialogue.

....

....

....

....

5.6 The Last Class

Extract 3

MRS ZHOU: Good morning, Mr Ling. Welcome back. Can I remind you about our conversation last year?

MR LING looks up.

MR LING: Which one?

MRS ZHOU: Concerning that screen and its **oddity**. (*MRS ZHOU points to a fabric screen hanging on the wall*). Never **activate** it again.

MR LING: But the students love it.

MRS ZHOU: It is **perturbing**, Mr Ling. I've arranged to have it removed at the end of the day.

MR LING: (*sadly*) Yes, Mrs Zhou.

> **oddity:** strangeness
> **activate:** to turn on
> **perturbing:** worrying

Challenge

4 When writing a script, it is important to select phrases and use stage directions to *show* the reader rather than tell them about the characters.

In your notebook, write approximately 15 lines of dialogue for the following scenes.

   a A father and son are travelling on a train to a large city. The son is excited. The father is stressed.

   b A shop worker is persuading a customer to buy the coat she has tried on. The customer likes it, but the coat is expensive.

73

6 Life stories

> 6.1 Childhood poems

> **Language focus**
>
> Rhyme and rhythm are key features of poetry. When writing about rhyme and rhythm, make sure you link them to the *meaning* of the poem and always show how they support the ideas in the poem. For example, the poem 'Night Mail' by W. H. Auden is about a train travelling through the night carrying letters and packages. Here are two lines from the poem:
>
> *Letters of thanks, letters from banks,*
>
> *Letters of joy from girl and boy*
>
> The rhythm of the lines sound like a train speeding along a track. Notice how the rhyme also makes the poem 'gallop'. Together, the rhythm and rhyme give a sense of speed and urgency to the poem. They support the ideas and content of the poem.

Focus

1 Fill in the missing rhyming words in the poem by William Butler Yeats. Remember that the first line rhymes with the second, the third line rhymes with the fourth, etc. Check your answers in the Learner's Book and correct them here if you got any wrong.

> ### The Song of the Old Mother
>
> I rise in the dawn, and I kneel and blow
>
> Till the seed of the fire flicker and ....
>
> And then I must scrub, and bake, and sweep,
>
> Till stars are beginning to blink and ....
>
> And the young lie long and dream in their bed
>
> Of the matching of ribbons, the blue and the ....

74

> And their day goes over in idleness,
> And they sigh if the wind but lift up a ....
> While I must work, because I am old
> And the seed of the fire gets feeble and ....

Practice

2. Look at these lines from the poem. The words in bold are where the main beats of the lines fall. What do you notice about many of the words? What do they emphasise?

    - *I **rise** in the **dawn**, and I **kneel** and **blow***
    - *And **then** I must **scrub**, and **bake**, and **sweep**,*
    - *And the **young** lie **long** and **dream** in their **bed***
    - *While I must **work**, **because** I am **old***

    ....

    ....

3. Read the following points and use them to write a brief explanation of the effect of rhyme and rhythm in 'The Song of the Old Mother'.

    - The poem is about the never-ending jobs the mother does.
    - The mother does the same jobs repetitively every day.
    - The poem is a song – as shown in the title.

    ....

    ....

    ....

    ....

    ....

6 Life stories

Challenge

Reread the poem 'Lullaby' by John Fuller.

> **Lullaby**
>
> Sleep little baby, clean as a nut,
> Your fingers uncurl and your eyes are shut.
> Your life was ours, which is with you.
> Go on your journey. We go too.
>
> The bat is flying round the house
> Like an umbrella turned into a mouse.
> The moon is astonished and so are the sheep:
> Their bells have come to send you to sleep.
>
> Oh be our rest, our hopeful start.
> Turn your head to my beating heart.
> Sleep little baby, clean as a nut,
> Your fingers uncurl and your eyes are shut.

4 Around the poem, make notes on the rhyme and rhythm. Then write a short summary of your ideas. Link your points to the meaning of the poem. Think about the title and situation being described.

....

....

....

....

....

> 6.2 Growing up

> **Language focus**
>
> The voice of a text means the personality or attitude of the person telling the story. The voice that writers choose depends on the purpose and audience of the text. For example, the voice in a text about a serious topic written for adults will usually be formal. A text written for a younger audience may have a less formal voice.
>
> The formality of a text is shown in the complexity of the words, sentence structures and punctuation a writer uses. Look at the difference in these two quotes: one is light-hearted and friendly and the other seems more formal and serious.
>
> *My friend Boo is brilliant! She's kind, funny and bright. I love her, but I also hate her. Just joking! She's great.* (from a children's novel)
>
> *I realised that I had grown apart from my childhood friends: to me, they now seemed aggressive and thoughtless.* (from an adult autobiography)

Focus

1 **a** Make notes on this paragraph, commenting on the content (what the text is about), the sentence types and the types of words the writer uses.

> I grew up in a small town in Canada. I had a lovely time growing up. Me and my friends spent a lot of time playing outside. I moved abroad as an adult. I miss my home town. I hope I will move back one day.

b Describe the voice of this paragraph. Focus on the words and sentence structures used.

....

....

6 Life stories

Practice

2   Read these two comments. Beneath each one, describe the voice. Is it formal? Funny? Friendly?

   a
   > Vancover is perhaps the most elegant city in the northern hemisphere and I would recommend a visit to anyone who has yet to visit it. Upon arriving, I was greeted by a sea of friendly faces. I settled into my hotel, which was situated in the heart of the city, and took it upon myself to explore this wonderful location. I was not disappointed.

   ....

   ....

   b
   > Vancouver is great! Go if you get the chance. I'd never been and couldn't wait to go there. The people are so friendly. I checked into my hotel and went out to explore. It was as good as I'd hoped.

   ....

   ....

3   Complete this table, giving three examples.

Complex words in A	Less complex words in B
1	1
2	2
3	3

Challenge

4 Read this extract from the biography of Malala Yousafzai. Rewrite it in a less formal voice for a younger audience. Change words and shorten sentences. You may also cut out some of the information.

> Growing up in Mingora, Malala would have got used to the crowded streets, which were increasingly populated by people moving in from local villages. Although the city is dirty in places, it is fascinating. Alongside shining new hotels, the local bazaar sells beautiful silk, precious gemstones and exotically scented candles. A stream weaves through the city, sadly polluted by plastic and other discarded material.

....

....

....

....

....

....

....

> 6.3 Leaving home

Some types of personal writing, such as autobiographies, present real experiences in a literary way. This makes the writing poetic and highly descriptive.

Focus

1 Read this extract, in which a man describes returning home after a trip overseas. Make notes around the extract, identifying literary and descriptive language that makes the writing sound poetic.

6 Life stories

> My plane was late, so by the time my taxi crawled sleepily into my street, I was ready for bed. But a strange thing happened as I saw my house. A rosy bird took flight somewhere in my heart. Home. A simple word for a beautiful concept. Home was where my family lived. The light above the door glowed, beckoning me home from my travels. 'Come,' it seemed to say, 'this is a place of love and safety.'

Practice

2   Read this extract. Choose two language techniques used in the extract and write about them. Explain the impact of the language and/or techniques used.

> I tiptoed inside my family home and was met by a beautiful silence. I was surprised and delighted to find my wife dozing in the chair by the warmth of the fire. Upstairs, my daughter slept on, travelling through the messy world of dreams. The house was sleeping, but in many ways, it was alive with the warmth of a quiet love.

Example 1: ....

....

....

....

Example 2: ....

....

....

....

Challenge

3   Write a paragraph in the style of an autobiography. Choose one of the following events in your life, or use an idea of your own:

- first day at school
- moving house
- an accident.

Remember to use interesting vocabulary and techniques to describe your real-life event.

....

....

....

....

....

....

....

....

> 6.4 Becoming a parent

Language focus

Writers use embedded clauses – clauses placed in the middle of sentences – to add detail and explanation to their writing. Commas are usually used to separate embedded clauses. For example:

As I walked down the lane, which was something I did every evening, I thought about you.

When I returned home, familiar though it was, I felt I didn't belong there.

6 Life stories

Focus

1. Highlight the embedded clauses in these examples from *Letter to Daniel* by Fergal Keane.

   a *Your mother, more tired yet more happy than I've ever known her, is sound asleep in the room next door and there is a soft quiet in our apartment.*

   b *Now, looking at your sleeping face, inches away from me, listening to your occasional sigh and gurgle, I wonder how I could have ever thought glory and prizes and praise were sweeter than life.*

Practice

Read this extract from another part of *Letter to Daniel*.

> Daniel, these memories explain some of the fierce protectiveness I feel for you, the tenderness and the occasional moments of blind terror when I imagine anything happening to you. But there is something more, a story from long ago that I will tell you face to face, father and son, when you are older. It's a very personal story but it's part of the picture. It has to do with the long lines of blood and family, about our lives and how we can get lost in them and, if we're lucky, find our way out again into the sunlight.

2. Underline two examples of embedded clauses in the extract you have just read.

3. What extra detail do the two embedded clauses add to the sentences they belong to?

   ....
   ....
   ....
   ....

Challenge

4. Write your own paragraph that uses embedded clauses to arrange information. You could write about one of the following ideas or choose one of your own:

- your feelings about a family member
- an account of a difficult situation
- arriving in a new town.

....

....

....

....

....

....

> 6.5 Exploring the world

Experimenting with different word orders and uses of punctuation can create different results and meaning in poetry.

Focus

These two poems have been created using from words from *Robert Scott's account of his last expedition* from 2 February 1911. The words have been put in a different order and different punctuation has been used.

On the Brink

The vast silence

The crevasse: the hidden danger

Struggling for foothold . . . on the brink . . .

. . . footsteps! The patter of dog pads! Conversation!

The sun. The gentle flutter of our canvas shelter.

Sleeping.

6 Life stories

The Hidden Danger!

The sun sleeping. The gentle flutter of our canvas shelter . . .

Footsteps . . . the patter of dog pads . . . conversation . . .

The crevasse!

Struggling for foothold

ON THE BRINK!

The . . .

       VAST . . .

              SILENCE.

1   Describe the differences in tone and meaning between the two poems.

   ……………………………………………………………………………………………

   ……………………………………………………………………………………………

   ……………………………………………………………………………………………

   ……………………………………………………………………………………………

   ……………………………………………………………………………………………

   ……………………………………………………………………………………………

   ……………………………………………………………………………………………

   ……………………………………………………………………………………………

   ……………………………………………………………………………………………

   ……………………………………………………………………………………………

   ……………………………………………………………………………………………

Practice

2 Here is another poem generated from Scott's diary. Change the word order and punctuation to create another version of the poem.

> **The Wind**
>
> Beneath the smoky cloud, the crisp ring of ponies' hoofs.
> Whine of dog, patter of dog pads, neigh of our steeds . . .
> The gentle flutter,
> Deep booming,
> Snow drift advancing . . .
> Yellow wraiths blotting out
> Floundering, clawing and struggling . . .
> The full force of a blizzard.

6 Life stories

Challenge

Here is another extract from Scott's diary. It recounts the terrible moment when Scott realises that his companion, Titus Oates, is very ill. Scott is suffering, too.

> **16 March 1912 or 17 March 1912**
>
> Tragedy all along the line. At lunch, the day before yesterday, poor Titus Oates said he couldn't go on; he proposed we should leave him in his sleeping-bag. That we could not do, and induced him to come on, on the afternoon march. In spite of its awful nature for him he struggled on and we made a few miles. At night he was worse and we knew the end had come.

3   How is the personal context of Scott reflected in this extract? How does the sentence structure and order reflect the immediate suffering he feels? Explain your thoughts with examples.

....

....

....

....

....

> 6.6 Changing the world

When planning and writing a speech, it is important to think about tone of voice and the sequence of your argument.

Focus

In the Practice section, you will read a speech about the importance of sport in schools. It is a speech given by a learner in a school assembly.

6.6 Changing the world

1 Which of these lines would make the most appropriate opening for the audience? Place a tick next to the one you think would be the most effective, then explain your choice.

   a   I bid you a fond good morning, my respected school friends and teachers. ☐

   b   Here's my speech about sport. You must listen. All of you. ☐

   c   Good morning everybody. I am going to talk about why sport is essential in school. ☐

   ....
   ....
   ....

Practice

Read the three paragraphs from the speech.

> Sport is, for me, the most important part of school life. I find I am good at most subjects – I enjoy them and am probably best at science. Science is a really worthwhile subject as I'm sure you'll agree. Everybody needs science whether they like it or not. But science is not like sport.
> I come alive when I play sport. When I am on the football pitch, nothing else matters. It's the place where I am truly me. When my shot hits the back of the net like a hammer, it's the best feeling ever.
>
> But it's not just about the enjoyment. Sport is a really good way to stay fit. We live in a world where obesity and poor health is increasing amongst teenagers. Some of us sit on our sofas watching TV, addicted to the screen. Playing sport gets people off their sofas and gives them a better quality of life. Whether you're a brilliant sportsperson or not, it doesn't matter – it's the exercise that is the important thing.
>
> Sport is like glue. It binds people together. Whether you play it or watch it, it's addictive. It's a great place to meet new friends. I met some of the best people I know playing sport. Sports people are definitely competitive, but they're also kind and supportive. Even when you're playing a really fierce game of football, when the whistle blows, everyone is a friend. Sport is powerful and a force for good.

6 Life stories

2 Summarise what each paragraph says. What are the main points covered?

Paragraph 1:

....

....

....

Paragraph 2:

....

....

....

Paragraph 3:

....

....

....

Which lines are the most effective in the speech? Give three examples and explain why you think they are effective.

....

....

....

....

....

....

Challenge

3 Write the final paragraph of the speech. In it, you must make the point that more people in your class should join sports teams. Use figurative language.

....

....

....

....

....

....

....

....

....

....

7 'The Travel Agency'

> 7.1 The picture gallery

> **Language focus**
>
> Writers choose adjectives and nouns carefully to describe situations and characters. Words are chosen to give precise information. Look at how these adjective and noun choices can offer different meanings:
>
> - The fierce thing approached me.
> - The angry kitten approached me.
> - The nasty cat approached me.
> - The snarling animal approached me.
>
> The order is important. When an adjective is placed first in a sentence, it emphasises the subject's quality (what it is like). When it is placed after the noun, the focus is on the object and can make the quality being described less important. For example:
>
> - The damaged car moved down the street.
> - The car, which was damaged, moved down the street.

Focus

1 Use two different colours to highlight the adjectives and nouns in these sentences.

   a   The horse ran through the green field.

   b   I was wearing a red coat.

   c   Abdul looked closely at his new book.

   d   The cat, which was furry and black, ran across the floor.

   e   I got off the train, which was old and smelly.

Practice

2 Fill in the gaps in the sentences with adjectives of your own choice. Think carefully about the effect your choices have.

    a The .... little entry bell overhead.

    b She peeled off her .... hood.

    c Hanna's trainers left .... wet footprints on the .... stone floor.

3   **a** Rewrite this sentence so the adjective comes after the noun:

Rain hammered against the window pane as she peeled off her sopping hood.

....

....

    b Which version of the sentence do you think works best? Why?

....

....

Challenge

4 Explain the impact of choice and positioning of adjectives in this extract from 'The Travel Agency' by Maria Turtschaninoff.

> She looked around and, for a second, wished she hadn't come. Behind a curved counter of light-blue glass a receptionist with blonde hair in a neat ponytail was talking on a mobile phone. Hanna's trainers left dirty wet footprints on the polished stone floor. She was definitely out of place.

....

....

....

....

7 'The Travel Agency'

> 7.2 The keys

Advertisements are written to persuade readers to buy products. Images are very important in adverts, but the language used is also an essential part of the promotion. Word choices and language techniques combine to make products seem exciting.

Focus

1. How effective do you find these phrases in persuading customers to buy a new phone? Rank the phrases in order of how persuasive you think they are from most persuasive to least persuasive.

   a 'The new Jphone 20 is powerful and compact.'

   b 'Expertly designed and beautifully made: the Jphone 20 is the only phone you need.'

   c 'You can buy a new Jphone 20 from lots of online retailers.'

   d 'The new Jphone 20 has lots of features which young people need.'

   ....

Practice

2. Read the following extract from a holiday brochure. Using different colours, highlight words and sentences that:
   - give factual information
   - are persuasive.

   > **Come to Bali**
   >
   > If you've never been to Bali before, you're missing out! Bali has everything that adventurous travellers could wish for. Whether you want to explore the culture of this piece of heaven on Earth, or whether you want to explore the thrilling landscape, we can promise a trip of a lifetime.
   >
   > The breathtaking scenery in the north boasts the dramatic mountains and sleeping volcanoes. The beaches of the south are paradise. A beautiful calmness blankets the island and serene temples nestle in the landscape. The islanders greet travellers as old friends. You will return from Bali a different person. What are you waiting for? Your trip to this truly magical island awaits.

3 Analyse the following sentences, explaining the techniques used and why they sound persuasive. Think about:

- direct address
- metaphor
- personification.

a *If you've never been to Bali before, you're missing out!*

....

....

....

b *The breathtaking scenery in the north boasts the dramatic mountains and sleeping volcanoes.*

....

....

....

c *The beaches of the south are paradise.*

....

....

....

d *A beautiful calmness blankets the island and serene temples nestle in the landscape.*

....

....

....

7 'The Travel Agency'

e *What are you waiting for?*

....

....

....

Challenge

4 Write a persuasive paragraph for each of these tasks. Think carefully about the words you choose. Use some of the language techniques you noticed in the previous activity.

a Write a paragraph attempting to persuade readers to visit a nearby town or city. You must make the place seem exciting and welcoming.

....

....

....

....

....

....

b Write a paragraph persuading new staff to join your school. You must focus on the interesting aspects of the school and the happy learners.

....

....

....

....

....

....

> 7.3 Hanna's friend

> **Language focus**
>
> Writers present heroic characters through their appearance and actions. Often the voice of a heroic story sounds 'elevated', as if the exciting qualities of the main character are reflected in the tone of the narrator. This example describes a brave character rescuing someone:
>
> *Ellis burst through the door, faster and stronger than an angry bull. He took one look at the hostage lying on the floor, grabbed him and burst out of the rear exit. Ellis Smith. A name to be admired and feared.*
>
> Notice the 'energy' of the writing, and language features, such as the simile and varied sentence types, which help to create a sense of drama around the character.

Focus

1. Underline words and phrases in the following extract that make the writer's uncle seem heroic.

> **Extract 1**
>
> My handsome uncle was born in Egypt in 1945. His family didn't have much money, but he never complained. He was always searching for a way to make his life better. When he was 16, he left his old life behind: he wanted a better one. As he walked out of his childhood home for the last time, he carried a huge suitcase in his powerful arms and looked straight ahead. Nobody could stop him from finding his dream.

7 'The Travel Agency'

Practice

Now read the next part of the story.

Extract 2

My earliest memory of my uncle is of a man who everybody looked up to. He was a larger-than-life character. He was as tall as a mountain and as kind as a nurse. As I grew up, he became more of a friend. He would visit our house every other day and stay for dinner. He had many great stories to tell about his travels. It seems that he got into some difficult situations, but always escaped unharmed and with a smile on his face.

There are very few photographs of my uncle as a younger man, but one of them, taken by my mother, shows how strong he was. In the photograph, he had just finished playing a game of football and stood there holding the ball in his arms. He had scored the winning goal in the local cup final. His team mates were cheering but he stood still, like a strong oak tree. It was only a few weeks after the picture was taken that he had his accident.

The accident happened as he was walking home from work. As he turned the corner, he saw a child crossing the street. The child was about to be struck by a car. My uncle bravely leapt to save the child. Luckily, the child was unharmed. Unfortunately, my uncle was seriously injured. It was the end of his football career, but he survived. In the years ahead, he came to live with us. He was like a ray of sunshine. He made us laugh and was happy despite his injuries.

I think my uncle is a fantastic man. Not only is he an interesting person with a fascinating history, he is also very special to me. My own father died before I was born and I have always thought of my uncle as the father I never had.

7.3 Hanna's friend

2 List all the heroic things that the writer's uncle has done in his life.

....

....

....

....

....

....

3 Write down four similes used to describe the uncle.

....

....

....

....

Challenge

4 In your notebook, write an account of a heroic character. Remember to describe the exciting and useful things they have done. Choose words carefully to make the character sound impressive. Try to use three similes in your account, and vary your sentence types to make your writing interesting and dramatic. Make sure your handwriting is neat and clear.

> 7 'The Travel Agency'

> 7.4 The fireplace

Knowing the names of the different word classes, as well as what function they serve in a sentence, is an important skill. It will help you understand different texts and to use language effectively in your own writing.

Focus

1   Draw a line to link the terms in the left-hand column to the correct definition in the right-hand column.

Term	Definition
adjective	shows the relationship between two nouns
adverb	describes an action
noun	a word which gives more detail about an action
preposition	the name of an object
verb	a word which gives more detail about a noun
conjunction	a word joining two clauses

Practice

2   Label the words in these sentences using the following abbreviations:
    adj (adjective); **adv** (adverb); **n** (noun); **p** (preposition); **v** (verb); **con** (conjunction).

   a   Hanna came in and closed the door behind her, setting off the piercing little entry bell overhead.

   b   Behind a curved counter of light-blue glass a receptionist with blonde hair in a neat ponytail was talking on a mobile phone.

   c   She placed a small sign with the words 'Ring for assistance' next to a brass bell on the counter and walked over to a frosted glass door.

   d   When she re-emerged she found herself no longer in the turquoise sea but in a cold grey sea bordered by smooth rocks.

Challenge

3   In your notebook, write an analysis of the way language is used in the following extract from 'The Travel Agency'.

Use the correct terminology and explain the effect of these language choices..

> She had made a friend there, in the other world, where the woods smelt like dark chocolate and the trees spun spells and weaved dreams between their branches. A friend the likes of which she had never had here, in this world of loneliness and rain and school and stinky sports halls. *Sannala*. Hanna held the name close to her heart like a glowing ember. The memory of Sannala was the only thing that kept Hanna warm through her cold everyday life. Sannala with her blue hair and skin like streaked granite.

> 7.5 Time

You may be asked to write a text using a personal voice. When you write a diary entry or a letter to a friend, it is important to choose the words and voice carefully. Often, these types of creative texts seem as if they are speaking directly to the reader.

Focus

1   Which two statements below have the most personal voice?
    Place a tick next to them.

   a   Walking along the street, I noticed a car moving quickly. Its occupants were young and I thought that something suspicious was going on. ☐

   b   I can't believe it! Today, I got home and opened the letter from you. What a surprise! It was all I had wished for. ☐

   c   Did I tell you about the time I lost my phone? It was when I'd got back from a holiday from Riyadh. I was sure I had it in my pocket when I got off the plane, but you know me – I'm a bit forgetful... ☐

   d   When buying a guitar, it's very important to make sure that the neck is straight. If it's not, it can affect the tuning and the problem is unlikely to be repaired. ☐

7 'The Travel Agency'

Practice

2 One way of creating a personal voice so the reader feels like you are addressing them in an informal way is by using exclamations or questions, almost as if you are 'talking' to the reader. Here is a line from 'The Travel Agency' describing Hanna's relationship with Sannala:

The memory of Sannala was the only thing that kept Hanna warm through her cold everyday life.

a Put yourself in the position of Hanna and imagine you are writing a diary entry. Rewrite the statement in a personal voice. You will need to rephrase it to show the emotion Hanna feels.

....

....

....

b Now rewrite the following line in a voice that expresses Hanna's admiration for Sannala.

Sannala who could talk to birds and who dived headlong into every new adventure with a hearty chuckle.

....

....

....

....

....

....

....

....

Challenge

3 Sannala never appears in the story – she is described through Hanna's memories. In your notebook, write a brief letter from Sannala to Hanna, based on the extracts you have read. You should mention their adventures and how you feel. Focus on capturing the emotions Sannala feels. Use an appropriate level of formality.

....

....

....

....

....

....

....

> 7.6 The beach

Themes are the big ideas that are explored several times and in different ways during a story. Interpreting themes and being able to track them across a story helps you to understand what a story means.

Focus

1 One of the themes of 'The Travel Agency' is friendship. Which two other themes are contained in the story? Place a tick next to two themes which the writer wants you to think about.

- **a** kindness ☐
- **b** politics ☐
- **c** power ☐
- **d** crime ☐
- **e** adventure ☐
- **f** death ☐

7 'The Travel Agency'

Practice

2 Another important theme in the story is loneliness and isolation. Here are some quotations that show these ideas in the story:

- *She looked around and, for a second, wished she hadn't come.*
- *She was definitely out of place.*
- *Hanna looked down at the floor, disappointed.*
- *The memory of Sannala was the only thing that kept Hanna warm through her cold everyday life.*
- *And she was alone . . .*

In your own words, explain what these quotations show about Hanna's circumstances and feelings.

....

....

....

....

....

3 Explain what happens at the end of the story to change Hanna's situation.

....

....

....

....

....

7.6 The beach

Challenge

4 Think carefully about how humans are shown in the story 'The Travel Agency' and what the writer suggests about them. Then explain how the writer shows the positive aspects of human nature.

    a   List six quotations from the story that show people doing good things.

....

....

....

....

....

....

....

    b   Explain what you think the writer is saying about human nature in the story.

....

....

....

....

....

....

....

8 In the city

> 8.1 The drama of Delhi

Language focus

Writers build up the detail in sentences in different ways. When doing so, they choose punctuation carefully not only to organise their sentences, but also to create particular effects.

- Commas can be used to build detail in lists and create emphasis, for example, 'the huge, shaggy, wild-eyed, angry bear'. This not only describes the bear in detail, but the long list separated by commas also creates an impression of the bear as being big and scary.

- Semi-colons are used to separate two clauses that are linked in terms of the ideas they express, for example, 'The bear lashed out; its sharp claws caught my arm.' Semi-colons are often used in more formal writing.

- Dashes can be used to add extra detail to a sentence. If they are used in the middle of a sentence, the parts on either side of the dashes should still make sense as a sentence if the bit in between the dashes is taken away, for example, 'The bear – which was huge and wild-eyed – began lumbering towards me.' A single dash can also be used to separate information for effect, for example, 'I had just one instinct – run!'

Focus

1 Rewrite these sentences adding punctuation where appropriate. Consider carefully where to use commas, dashes, colons and semi-colons.

   a   As a doctor the most common illnesses I treat are coughs childhood infections and high blood pressure.

   ....

   ....

b When I went to university I took several things my laptop my speakers a recipe book.

....

....

c The night was dark starry and exciting.

....

....

d My father's farm has pigs sheep and bulls.

....

....

Practice

Writers choose different punctuation for different effects. For example, they may choose commas to separate clauses, or they may use dashes or brackets instead.

2 Rewrite the following extract. Use other forms of punctuation instead of dashes where possible.

> There was a fierce jam on the road to Gurgaon. Every five minutes the traffic would tremble – we'd move a foot – hope would rise – then the red lights would flash on the cars ahead of me, and we'd be stuck again.

....

....

....

....

8 In the city

Challenge

3 Now practise writing your own sentences using commas to separate the detail. Use the following for ideas.

- You are running through an airport. You are late for the flight and desperate to make it in time.
- A teenager is walking quickly through the rain to get to a friend's house.
- A man is lying on the grass. He is enjoying the sunshine and all the sights and sounds around him.

....

....

....

....

....

....

....

> 8.2 The delights of Doha

The type of voice used in articles depends on its topic, purpose and audience. For example, an informative article about a serious topic will be written in a more formal voice than one on a light-hearted topic. An informative article written for children will use a less formal voice.

Focus

Here are two extracts taken from informative articles.

> **A**
>
> My guitar seriously rocks! I bought it from a friend and fell in love with it straight away. Plug it in and it sings like a bird. It might be old (like my father) and it'll get older (like my father), but it's one fine piece of wood (unlike my father!). What else does a boy need? With this beauty strapped to my neck, I can fly. Check it out in the pics. It's a killer.

> **B**
>
> Purchasing my new car took a tremendous amount of research. The first stage was to explore all the available reviews and compare vehicles: how much petrol it uses, safety and reliability are essential for me. Once I had decided on the type of car I wanted, I visited several showrooms and sought advice from knowledgeable colleagues.

1 Which extract uses the most formal voice? Which one uses the least formal?

   Most formal voice: extract ……

   Least formal voice: extract ……

2 Highlight words, phrases and punctuation in the extracts that show the level of formality.

Practice

Informative articles usually have a friendly, less formal tone – written in a way that makes the reader feel they are being helped by a more knowledgeable, approachable person.

8 In the city

3   Read the following example from a travel website, 'Things to Do in Doha', and highlight examples of words and phrases that direct the reader in a friendly way.

> Remember that in the holy month of **Ramadan**, most of the shopping complexes and commercial areas will be slow or shut for some time. So, it is better to avoid travelling during the month of Ramadan. You can check online for the month of Ramadan in the year you are planning to travel to Doha as it keeps changing every year depending on the Islamic calendar.

Ramadan: the ninth month of the Islamic year, during which strict fasting is observed from dawn to sunset.

Challenge

Voice can also be detected in the way that articles present detail. To convey a confident, helpful voice, the detail given is usually clear and thorough.

4   In your notebook, write two paragraphs that use different voices to convey information. Remember to think about word choices and punctuation to construct a voice. Start by thinking about the 'personality' of the writing. Here are some headings to help you, or you could choose your own:

   • How to cope when starting a new school
   • The history of space travel
   • The rules of basketball
   • How the internet was invented.

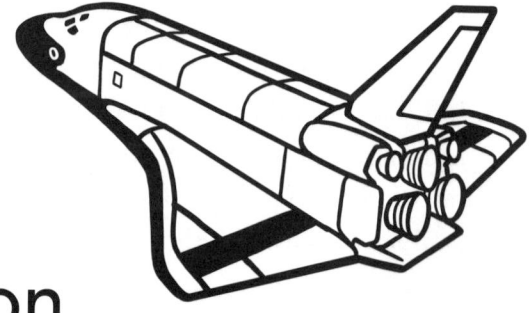

> 8.3 Mysterious London

Writers use conflict and problems to make their plots exciting and move the story along. The conflicts faced by characters are either with other characters, the surrounding situations or sometimes within themselves – an inner conflict. Settings and dialogue can reveal these conflicts.

Focus

1   Read the extract from *Neverwhere* by Neil Gaiman. Note the inner conflict the character Richard experiences. Make notes on:

   • what Richard wants
   • how he feels.

108

8.3 Mysterious London

Extract 1

Richard stared at the glistening street. It all seemed so normal, so quiet, so sane. For a moment, he felt that all he needed to get his life back would be to hail a taxi and tell it to take him home. And then he would sleep the night through in his own bed. But a taxi would not see him or stop for him, and he had nowhere to go, even if one did.

'I'm tired,' he said.

....
....
....
....
....

Practice

2   Now read another extract from *Neverwhere*, which reveals a conflict between Richard and the characters Door, Hunter and the Marquis. Highlight words and phrases that show the conflict.

109

8 In the city

> **Extract 2**
>
> No one said anything. Door would not meet his eyes, the Marquis was cheerfully ignoring him. He felt like a small child, unwanted, following the bigger children around, and that made him irritated. 'Look,' he said. 'I don't want to be a bother or anything. I know you are all very busy people. But what about me?'
>
> The Marquis turned and stared at him, eyes huge and white in his dark face. 'You?' he said. 'What about you?'
>
> 'Well,' said Richard. 'How do I get back to normal again? It's like I've walked into a nightmare. Last week everything made sense, and now nothing makes sense . . . ' He trailed off. Swallowed. 'I want to know how to get my life back,' he explained.
>
> 'You won't get it back travelling with us, Richard,' said Door. 'It's going to be hard enough for you anyway. I . . . I really am sorry.'

Challenge

3   In your notebook, explain how the writer creates a sense of conflict in this next extract from *Neverwhere*. You should consider:

   • the effect of the strange setting

   • what is implied about Richard's feelings

   • the use of dialogue.

> **Extract 3**
>
> It smelled like drains at the top of the sewer – a dead, soapy, cabbagey smell. Grey water ran, shallow but fast, along the bottom of the brick tunnel. Richard stepped into it. He could see the lights of the others up ahead, and he ran and splashed down the tunnel until he caught up with them.
>
> 'Go away,' said the Marquis.
>
> 'No,' he said.
>
> Door glanced up at him. 'I am really sorry, Richard,' she said.
>
> The Marquis stepped between Richard and Door. 'You can't go back to your old home or your old job or your old life,' he said to Richard, almost gently. 'None of those things exist. Up there, *you* don't exist.'

> 8.4 Bringing the city to life

Language focus

Writers often describe settings in a way that makes them come to life. For example, they use figurative language such as personification. Personification means giving human qualities to non-human objects. For example:

- The city belched out poisonous smoke.
- The road slithered through the city.

One of the main effects of personification is to create a sense of excitement or threat. For example, writers might personify a large, imposing building as 'gazing down' at the narrator. This might imply that the narrator feels threatened.

Focus

1 Tick the statements below that are examples of personification. There are three in total.

   a   The boy threw the pen across the room. It danced gracefully and twisted in the air then landed with a thud on the carpet. ☐

   b   As I walked out of the door, it closed with a bang. The dog whimpered and my little brother looked scared as we headed out into the unknown. ☐

   c   It had started to rain heavily. There were people on the streets and the air was as cold as a freezer. Amina knew that a storm would happen. Where could she find shelter? ☐

   d   The exam started and my nerves increased. Everything was against me. The exam paper stared back at me, daring me to open it. I had revised so hard. I had to pass this exam. ☐

   e   As Ron entered the hall, the clock growled at him. He was late. Very late. What would he say to Mrs Smith? This was going to be a very bad day indeed. ☐

8 In the city

Practice

2 Writers use a range of techniques in combination to describe settings. Read this extract from *Dr Jekyll and Mr Hyde* by Robert Louis Stevenson, written in the 19th century. It uses several techniques to describe a city, including personification. Using different colours, highlight the following techniques:

- simile
- personification
- alliteration.

> It was a fine, dry night; frost in the air; the streets as clean as a ballroom floor; the lamps, unshaken, by any wind, drawing a regular pattern of light and shadow. By ten o'clock, when the shops were closed, the by-street was very solitary and, in spite of the low growl of London from all round, very silent. Small sounds carried far; domestic sounds out of the houses were clearly audible on either side of the roadway.

Challenge

3 In your notebook, describe a distinctive setting. Focus on using personification in your writing. Use other types of figurative language if you can. You could use one of these ideas or come up with your own:

- an empty schoolroom during a holiday
- a river at night time
- a busy beach in hot weather.

> 8.5 City problems

Language focus

Words have related forms. For example, the word 'unique' (an adjective) also has forms such as 'uniquely' (adverb) and 'uniqueness' (noun). Being able to identify the root word can help you work out what is meant when prefixes and suffixes are added. Understanding the etymology of a word can also help you to understand other words.

8.5 City problems

Focus

1 Draw a circle around the root word in each list.

   a happiest   happy   unhappy   happier   happily
   b behave   behaving   misbehaviour behaviour   misbehaved
   c legality   illegal   illegality   legal   legally
   d maturely   immature   mature   immaturity   maturity

Practice

2 Make brief notes about the etymology of the following words.
   Use a dictionary to help you.

   a indicate

      ....

      ....

   b television

      ....

      ....

   c weather

      ....

      ....

Challenge

3 The following passage contains some words in bold which may be unfamiliar to you. Use the context of the sentence and recognisable parts of the word to help you write a definition. Check your answers in the dictionary and note the etymology of each word.

8 In the city

> **Dirty Cities**
> What can be done to **alleviate** the problem of dirty cities? If we could **eliminate** or even just **stabilise** fossil fuel **emissions**, that would be a start. Action is needed to **minimise** our **dependency** on fossil fuels, but we will also need to **acclimatise** to **impending** changes.

a alleviate

   ....

b eliminate

   ....

c stabilise

   ....

d emissions

   ....

e minimise

   ....

f dependency

   ....

g acclimatise

   ....

h impending

   ....

> 8.6 City solutions

> **Language focus**
>
> Writers choose the 'angle' they tell things from. One of the key decisions is whether to use the first-, second- or third-person perspective. First-person writing makes it seem as if you are seeing things through the narrator's eyes – as a reader, you get direct access to the narrator's thoughts and ideas. Second-person perspective is not often used. This is where the writer addresses the reader as 'you'. Third-person perspective is where a narrator describes what is happening to characters. In this perspective, the reader does not hear things from a single character. Instead, the narrator can explain the action from a distance. Most stories are written in the third person, although many are told in the first person.

Focus

1 Which perspective are these statements written from?
   Write first, second or third next to each one.

Statement	Which person?
You wake up early because you have a very important interview. You get washed, get dressed and leave the house in a hurry, not sure what the day will bring.	
Although my sister Hannah didn't want me to, I took her shopping. Our mother had told me to not let Hannah out of my sight all day.	
As the car came screaming around the corner, Leon just made it onto the pavement. The driver stopped, stared menacingly at Leon and drove off.	
She wasn't expecting anything, so when the headteacher called her name and Umma collected her award, she was astounded.	
Once the sun came out, you ran outside and enjoyed the feeling of heat on your face. You would spend every day like this if you could.	
I was planning to spend the day playing on my computer, but my dad had other ideas. My dad wanted me to tidy my room and help out with some decorating. It was the last thing I wanted.	

8 In the city

Practice

2   Rewrite the following paragraphs, changing the perspective from first person to third person. You will have to think about names and how you might rearrange sentences completely.

> **When I Met Hassan**
>
> This was my city. The whole glorious and slightly frightening city was my playground. As I walked along the main street, I looked in the shop windows at the reflections of beautiful architecture. I'd walked down here thousands of times, but I was also delighted to see the tall, old buildings staring kindly at me. As I turned the corner, it was a surprise to bump into my old friend, Hassan. 'Hey,' I said. 'How are you?'
>
> Hassan smiled. 'I'm very well. How long has it been since we met?' he asked me. We spent the afternoon walking through the city, chatting about the old days and our families. It was the most brilliant afternoon I had spent in the most brilliant city.

Challenge

3   It is useful to practise writing in the second person. Write a paragraph that uses the second person throughout. Start your paragraph with this sentence:

You finally got home after a long day and you couldn't believe your eyes. On the table was a letter that would change your life. ....

....

....

....

....

....

....

....

....

9 Dangers of the sea

> 9.1 Jaws

> **Language focus**
>
> Writers choose words and phrases to portray the appearance and manner of their characters. By using language carefully to suggest small details such as colours, sounds and movement, writers can imply things about their characters' personality and attitudes. For example, the following description of a wolf uses words and phrases to suggest certain qualities about the animal:
>
> > *As it came around the corner, the deep black eyes of the animal seemed to get darker. The wolf stopped and stood completely still. Now and again, its nose twitched. It stared. Slowly, it crouched, waiting to pounce. Its jaw opened slightly and as it leapt, it let out a fierce growl from its black throat.*
>
> The use of dark colours suggests something dangerous about the wolf. The words used to describe movement are contrasting: they focus on the stillness of the animal, which seems threatening, and then the verb 'leapt' suggests the wolf's power. Its growl is described as 'fierce', which also suggests dangerous power. Together, these words present an animal that appears threatening and fearsome.

Focus

1 Look at the following phrases. What do they suggest about the sea creature being described?
Think about how the words suggest personality and/or attitude.
Complete the table.

9.1 Jaws

Sentence	What is being suggested
The sea-horse glided majestically through the water.	The use of 'glided' implies a gracefulness about the creature. 'Majestically' has connotations of power and status.
The sunlight pierced the water revealing the beautiful blue and green scales of the fish.	
Slowly and menacingly, the lobster plotted its way along the sea bed.	

Practice

2   Read the following extract about Hooper's encounter with the shark in *Jaws* by Peter Benchley. Underline key words and phrases that suggest the shark's power and personality.

> The fish slid backward out of the cage and turned sharply to the right in a tight circle. Hooper then saw the wide gap in the bars and saw the giant head **lunging** through it. He raised his hands above his head, grasping at the escape **hatch**.
>
> The fish **rammed** through the space between the bars, spreading them still farther with each thrust of its tail. Hooper, flattened against the back of the cage, saw the mouth reaching, straining for him. He remembered the head, and he tried to lower his right arm and grab it. The fish thrust again.

lunging: moving downwards quickly and forcefully
hatch: a small entrance
rammed: pushed violently

Write a paragraph explaining how the writer's word choices create an impression of the shark's power.

- Clearly state the impression created.
- Use the examples you have found, commenting on the effect created.
- Identify word classes and language techniques.

9 Dangers of the sea

....

....

....

....

....

Challenge

3   Invent a new type of sea creature. Start by imagining its size, shape and colour. Is it threatening or beautiful? What name would you give it? Write a description of your creature, focusing on small details such as colours, sounds and movement. Choose words and phrases that will give your reader a sense of the creature's qualities and appearance.

....

....

....

....

....

> 9.2 Victims and villains

One of the structural decisions a writer has to make is what each character knows about the situation they are in. They also need to choose how much information to give the reader. For example, if the reader knows that a character is in danger, it creates tension – especially if the character is unaware of it.

9.2 Victims and villains

Focus

1 Here are three paragraphs from a short story about a sailor. In the right-hand column, note down what information is kept from the reader in each paragraph. The first one has been done for you.

Paragraph content	What information the reader doesn't know
1 A sailor receives a letter telling him to arrive at the harbour to get on his boat the following morning with a packed suitcase.	Who the sailor is; why he has been sent the letter; who has sent it.
2 The sailor meets a friend that evening. They talk about a dangerous sea captain they both know. The friend knows a secret about the sea captain.	
3 The next morning, the sea captain is waiting on the ship in the harbour. He has an angry look on his face. The sailor hasn't arrived.	

Practice

2 Read the following story. Identify what the boy (Will), his father (Peter) and the reader do and do not know in each paragraph. Complete the table.

> As he walked home from school, Will wondered what his dad was doing. His dad, Peter, had gone on a business trip and was due to be away for another six months. Will missed his dad. He loved his mother, but his dad was like an older, cool brother.
>
> When Will was young, his family had moved to a large, beautiful house. It had cost a lot of money, and his dad had taken a well-paid job, which meant lots of time away from home. However, as Will walked home from school, he didn't know that at that very moment, his dad was sitting at home. It was Will's birthday and Peter had flown home to surprise him.
>
> Will pushed through the door and put his schoolbag down. As he walked into the room, there was his dad, arms wide open. Will ran into them and shed a quiet tear. Peter did too, but Will didn't notice. It was a great surprise, but Peter had an even bigger one for Will – next month, he was returning for good.

9 Dangers of the sea

Paragraph	Will's knowledge	Peter's knowledge	Reader's knowledge
1			
2			
3			

Challenge

3   Write a paragraph featuring two characters who know different things about a situation. You could set it at sea or somewhere else. Start by choosing a situation and characters. For example, it could be a teacher and a learner discussing missing homework. Remember you need to decide how much to tell the reader.

....

....

....

....

....

....

> 9.3 Fear!

In an informative article, paragraphs may serve different purposes. For example, the opening paragraph is often designed to 'hook' the reader – to attract their interest and make them want to read on. Later paragraphs might be intended to give readers advice.

Focus

Sentences containing advice can be written as imperatives (also called directives or commands). These are sentences that give orders. The subject is usually left out of an imperative sentence ('Wear a life jacket') but sometimes the subject is included ('You must wear a life jacket').

1   Read the following six sentences. Tick the three imperative sentences.

- Never pick up a jellyfish. ☐
- Whales are huge sea creatures. ☐
- The sea covers much of the globe. ☐
- Always take care when swimming. ☐
- We must look after our planet. ☐
- Should we go sailing? ☐

Practice

2   Advice can also be given in a less direct way. Read this article about facing your fears. Underline the key pieces of advice.

Overcoming Your Fears

Everybody has things they fear. It might be animals, small spaces or the dark. How can you overcome these fears? There's no easy solution but you might start by talking about them. Rather than pretending your fears don't exist, talk to a friend about them. Find a comfortable place and explain clearly how you feel. You could also explore why you are afraid – did something happen to make you feel that way? Is there a logical reason for your fear?

9 Dangers of the sea

A more extreme way to face your fear is to face it. To do this, you need to be very brave. If you're frightened of the dark, spend short amounts of time with the lights off. Remember to breathe and remember that you are in control. Another way of confronting your fears is to write about them. There are plenty of people with similar fears. Why not find others online who share your worries and help each other? If your fears are really affecting your life, remember that your doctor will always be able to offer advice and further support.

Challenge

3   Taking information and condensing it into notes is an important skill. To do this, you must make sure you understand the main ideas of a text.

Read the following extract from an article by Elaina Zachos, which gives a different view of sharks to the ones you have read so far. You should:

- identify the main reasons why humans should not view sharks as dangerous villains
- use this information to write a paragraph in your notebook titled 'A different view of sharks'.

Why are we afraid of sharks?

The number of shark attacks per year is increasing, but this isn't in line with the **skyrocketing** human population. Of the 80-odd shark attacks that happen each year, **fatality** rates are decreasing.

It's difficult to count sharks says Blake Chapman, a shark expert, but it appears their numbers are decreasing. To meet the demand for shark fin soup, some fishermen in Asia will catch sharks, chop off their fins, and then release them back into the water to die.

Studies have shown that shark populations can have an effect on sea grass composition and the presence of other animals in a habitat. Sharks are also being studied for cancer treatments.

skyrocketing: increasing in huge numbers
fatality: death

9.4 A tale of a whale

When written accurately and realistically, dialogue can bring stories and characters to life.

Focus

1 Write down four rules for setting out speech.

　　..

　　..

　　..

　　..

Practice

2 Dialogue can reveal information and show relationships between characters. It can indicate who is in charge and how characters are feeling.

- Underline all the dialogue in this extract of *And The Ocean Was Our Sky* by Patrick Ness.
- Complete the table to show what the dialogue reveals about the personalities and emotions of the three characters.

> 'Bathsheba!' the Captain called from what was now below me. 'Has he recovered?'
>
> 'He recovers from his drowning,' I answered. 'I don't know if he will ever recover from his fright.'
>
> I circled the young male. He still, remarkably held the disc in his hand, as if he'd forgotten it in his shock. He watched me, his eyes wide. I opened my mouth to bring him back –
>
> 'No, please!' he shouted.
>
> I was so surprised to be addressed directly I paused. Men rarely bothered to speak to us. They *never* spoke to Apprentices.
>
> 'You're going to kill me,' he gasped.

9 Dangers of the sea

Character	What the dialogue reveals about them
The Captain	
Bathsheba	
The young male	

Challenge

3   A writer has to decide which parts of their story to tell through dialogue and which parts to narrate. Rewrite the following examples of narrated stories to include dialogue. You will have to use your imagination!

   a   I looked at Jamil angrily. He told me the real reason why he no longer wanted to be my friend. I told him how that made me feel.

   ....

   ....

   ....

   ....

b I asked my friend to tell me her favourite memory from her childhood. She told me about a trip she went on at school.

....

....

....

....

c Chen directed the boat into the storm. Jian was worried and asked him lots of questions. Chen answered some of them.

....

....

....

....

> 9.5 The Rime of the Ancient Mariner 1

In *The Rime of the Ancient Mariner* by Samuel Taylor Coleridge, the poet offers vivid details about the Mariner's appearance, the wedding guest and the suffering of the sailors.

Focus

1 The opening of *The Rime of the Ancient Mariner* describes how the Mariner meets the wedding guest. Annotate the following lines to note what you discover about the Mariner's appearance.

> It is an ancient Mariner,

9 Dangers of the sea

> By thy long grey beard and glittering eye–

> He holds him with his skinny hand,

> Hold off! unhand me, grey-beard **loon**'

loon: madman

Practice

2   The Mariner's tale contains some terrible moments for the sailors. Annotate the following stanzas to show the physical effects the journey has on the Mariner and other sailors.

Extract 1

There passed a **weary** time. Each throat
Was **parched**, and **glazed** each eye.
A weary time! a weary time!
How glazed each weary eye,

With throats **unslaked**, with black lips baked,
We could nor laugh nor **wail**;
Through **utter drought** all **dumb** we stood!
I bit my arm, I sucked the blood,
And cried, A sail! a sail!

weary: tired
parched: dry; really thirsty
glazed: like glass
unslaked: dry
wail: cry
utter drought: absolute dryness
dumb: unable to speak

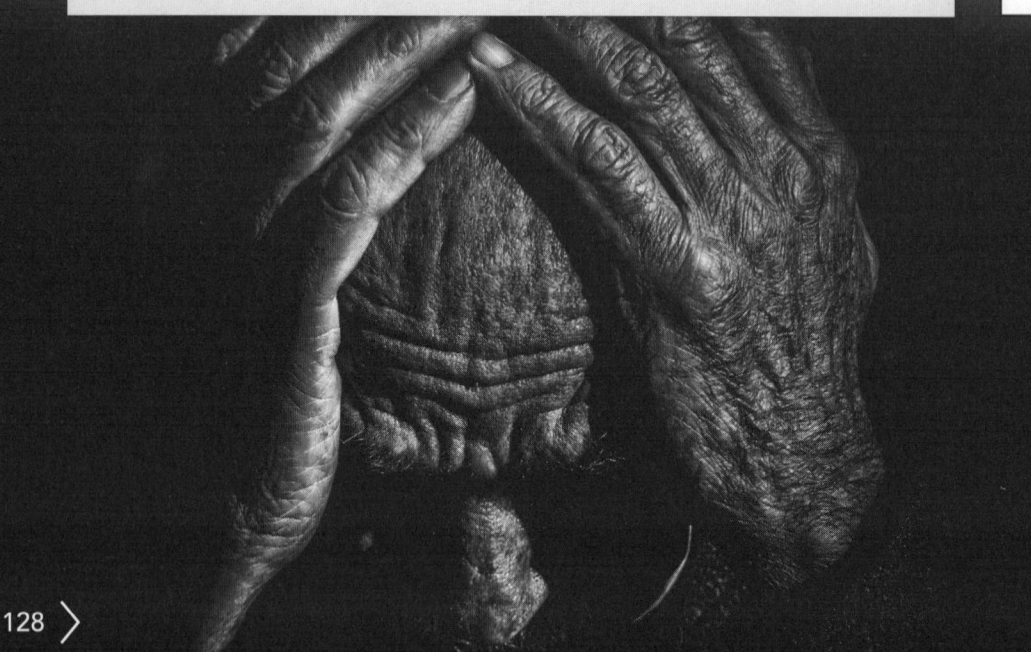

Challenge

3 In the following stanzas, the wedding guest talks to the Mariner about what he has heard so far. Look closely at the reaction of the guest, the appearance of the Mariner and what he says about his feelings. In your notebook, rewrite these stanzas as a story from the guest's point of view. You should start with:

I looked at the old man and trembled with fear.

> **Extract 2**
>
> 'I fear thee, ancient Mariner!
> I fear thy skinny hand!
> And **thou art** long, and **lank**, and brown,
> As is the **ribbed** sea-sand.
>
> I fear thee and thy **glittering** eye,
> And thy skinny hand, so brown.'—
> Fear not, fear not, thou Wedding-Guest!
> This body dropt not down.

thou art: you are
lank: thin
ribbed: wrinkled
glittering: shining brightly

> 9.6 The Rime of the Ancient Mariner 2

Language focus

Poets often use language techniques such as alliteration, rhyme, sibilance and assonance to make their poems sound interesting and memorable when read aloud. These techniques can also be used to support the meanings of the poem. For example, *All in a hot and copper sky* uses assonance. The 'o' sounds in 'hot' and 'copper' seem to emphasise the torture the Mariner is feeling. The sounds are long – they are drawn out when spoken, just like the drawn-out nature of the Mariner's suffering.

9 Dangers of the sea

Focus

1 Explore how rhyme varies in the poem. Annotate the poem to indicate the rhyme scheme, giving rhyming lines the same letter. The first stanza has been done for you.

Extract 3

And soon I heard a roaring wind:	A
It did not come **anear**;	B
But with its sound it shook the sails,	C
That were so thin and **sere**.	B

And the coming wind did roar more loud,
And the sails did sigh like **sedge**,
And the rain poured down from one black cloud;
The Moon was at its edge.

The thick black cloud was **cleft**, and still
The Moon was at its side:
Like waters shot from some high crag,
The lightning fell with never a jag,
A river steep and wide.

anear: close
sere: dry
sedge: a grass-like plant
cleft: split

2 Explain what happens in the story when the rhyme scheme changes in the third stanza.

....

....

....

....

130

9.6 *The Rime of the Ancient Mariner 2*

Practice

3 Read the following stanza, in which the Mariner describes watching the water snakes.
Highlight examples of sibilance and alliteration in this stanza.

> **Extract 4**
>
> Beyond the shadow of the ship,
> I watched the water-snakes:
> They moved in tracks of shining white,
> And when they **reared**, the **elfish** light
> Fell off in **hoary** flakes.

reared: rose up
elfish: mysterious
hoary: white like frost

4 Explain what happens in the story during this stanza.

....

....

....

Challenge

5 Explain the effect of sibilance and alliteration in Activity 3.
Focus on the atmosphere created by these techniques. Use examples to support your ideas.

....

....

....

....

....

> Acknowledgements

The authors and publisher acknowledge the following sources of copyright material and are grateful for the permissions granted. While every effort has been made, it has not always been possible to identify the sources of all the material used, or to trace all copyright holders. If any omissions are brought to our notice, we will be happy to include the appropriate acknowledgements on reprinting.

Unit 1: Excerpt from *Beware Low-Flying Girls* by Katherine Rundell. Published by Alma Books, 2017. Copyright © Katherine Rundell. Reproduced by permission of the author c/o Rogers, Coleridge & White Ltd., 20 Powis Mews, London W11 1JN; Excerpts from *Around India in 80 Trains* by Monisha Rajesh, reproduced with the permission of Hodder & Stoughton, Copyright © Monisha Rajesh; Excerpts from *Silverfin* by Charlie Higson, reproduced with the permission of Hachette Book Group and Curtis Brown on behalf of the Ian Fleming Literary Estate; **Unit 2:** 'Hey You Down There' by Harold Rolseth; **Unit 3:** except from 'Film Boy' by Alexander McCall Smith from *Stories of the World* compiled by Federation of Children's Book Groups; **Unit 4:** 'Tube-strike Haiku' by Rober McGough, used with the permission of United Agents; **Unit 5:** Excerpt(s) from *Wonder* by R. J. Palacio, copyright © 2012 by R. J. Palacio. Used by permission of Alfred A. Knopf, an imprint of Random House Children's Books, a division of Penguin Random House LLC. All rights reserved. Reprinted by permission of R.J. Palacio; **Unit 6:** John Fuller, 'Lullaby' from *Collected Poems*, published by Chatto & Windus. Used by permission of The Random House Group Limited; Excerpt from *Letter to Daniel: Despatches from the Heart* by Fergal Keane, BBC Books 1996; **Unit 7:** 'The Travel Agency' by Maria Turtschaninoff translated by A. A. Prime, abridged, used with kind permission; **Unit 8:** 'Things to do in Doha', used with the permission of AS Traveler https://astraveler.com/; Excerpts from *Neverwhere* by Neil Gaiman, used with the permission of Hachette Children Book and Writers House LLC; **Unit 9:** exctracts from *Jaws* by Peter Benchley, Copyright © 1974, Renewed 2002, Benchely IP, LLC. All Rights Reserved. Reproduced with permission of the Licensor through PLSclear; Text Copyright © 2018 Patrick Ness from AND THE OCEAN WAS OUR SKY written by Patrick Ness and Illustrated by Rovina Cai. Reproduced by permission of Walker Books Ltd London SE11 5HJ www.walker.co.uk and by permission of HarperCollins Publishers.

Thanks to the following for permission to reproduce images:

Cover image: paper sculpture created by Justin Rowe; *Inside:* **Unit 1:** Grafissimo/GI; José Moreira/GI; Teo Lannie/GI; Saudemont Hervé/GI; Tdubphoto/GI; Nina Vartanava/GI; Clare Jackson/EyeEm/GI; Tdubphoto/GI **Unit 2:** Natalia Zakharchenko/GI; Praveenkumar Palanichamy/GI; Robert-Andre Roszik/GI; Deimagine/GI; Fairfax Media Archives/GI; Cavan Images/GI; **Unit 3:** CSA Images/GI (x2); Silver Screen Collection/GI; Universal History Archive/GI; **Unit 4:** David Q. Cavagnaro/GI; Westend61 - FotoFealing/GI; C T Aylward/GI; Pioneer111/GI; Howard Kingsnorth/GI;BJI/Blue Jeans Images/GI; 4x6/GI; Lineacurves/GI **Unit 6:** PhotoAlto/GI; John M Lund Inc/GI; CSA Images/GI (x2); Whitemay/GI; Sdi Productions/GI; **Unit 7:** CSA Images/GI; FrankRamspott/GI; CSA Images/GI; Maurizio Brazzoduro/GI; **Unit 8:** CSA-Archive/GI; Dang Nguyen/GI; GeorgePeters/GI; CSA Images/GI; Yousef Alkh/GI; **Unit 9:** Nastasic/GI; Eriq Zain/GI; András Kozári/GI; Daniele Errico/GI; Duncan1890/GI

Key: GI= Getty Images.

The author would like to thank the following people for their support: Sarah Elsdon, Florence Kemsley, Sonya Newland, Rosalyn Scott and Naomi Sklar.